SEAN

LEARY'S

GREATEST

HITS

VOLUME ELEVEN:

OF TIME TRAVELERS AND TIKTOKS

THE

COVID

YEARS

PART TWO:

TIME TRAVELERS

AND TIKTOK

The columns of 2021, part one
January-April

This book is published in the United States by Dreaming World Books and Dreams Reach Productions.

ISBN is 978-1-948662-08-6

Library of Congress # Applied for.

Cover photo and design by Sean Leary.

Special thanks to Julius Cortez, PEPPING!, PB, TS Patti, Steve and Anne Holmes, Tess Abney, Tristan Tapscott, Khalil Hacker, Jonathan Turner, and everyone who has helped contribute to the success of QuadCities.com from the time I got there in January 2016 until present day.

It's been a great ride... let's keep enjoying the trip!

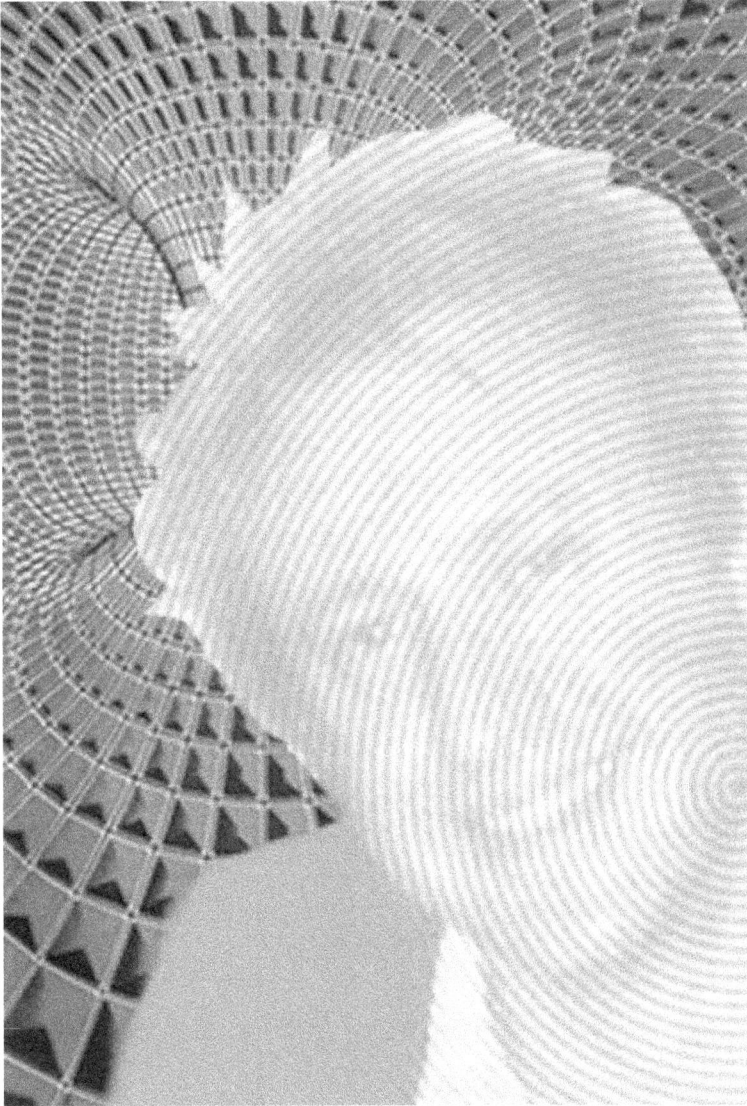

CONTENTS

Is Something HUGE Happening TOMORROW? This TIME TRAVELER FROM 2485 Says So...

Dec. 31, 2020

I hope you're stocked up on pizza rolls and champagne!

Because a HUGE WORLD EVENT is going to happen TOMORROW.

How do I know?

A time traveler told me.

Yup, that's right.

A time traveler.

No, I haven't been out to the Milan dispensary this morning, I'm talking about a person calling themselves @thatonetimetraveler on TikTok, who claims to be from the year 2485, where their company, Aura, has built the first functioning time machine.

The time traveler, who also claims to be human and from the planet Vadho (you know, where Cardi B and Megan Thee Stallion built that house), has been posting on TikTok for several months, and one of the things they've posted repeatedly is that something HUGE is going to happen on Jan. 2, 2021, which is a "very good and exciting day for humanity."

So, you're saying we're FINALLY going to get another Psy record???

Fingers crossed. I really NEED to whoop 'em Gangham Style again, but in a NEW 2021 Gangham Style. Yocha keeps trolling me about only whooping 2019 style.

Here are some other things of interest that @thatonetimetraveler has also opined on:

The monoliths that were appearing around the world throughout the fall have no meaning and were installed by humans who were using them as a joke and a publicity stunt. (I agree. I think it was the Burger King.)

In 2021, a group of people are going to discover a bunker from around 600 years ago that contains blueprints and inventions from our modern time that were apparently brought here more than six centuries ago from beings from another dimension. (Hmmm… iffy. We'll see… my guess is that they discover a bunker from 40 years ago that has a bunch of old Playboys in it, and an unopened can of Hamms…)

On July 9, 2025 the biggest hurricane ever starts up the East Coast. (THIS is a startling prediction? Bring your A game, time traveler! Tell us that it gets started when Godzilla farts or something!)

In 2026, forest fires become a huge threat to humanity, starting May 18 in Australia. (This one is not exactly a daring prediction; I can see that happening already, because nobody listens to Smokey the Bear anymore. Bastards.)

On Oct. 11, 2029 a gigantic planet explodes and is able to be observed from earth. (Again, not exactly daring here, dudeski. Telescopes on earth can see explosions throughout the universe all the time. BFD… c'mon, let's bring some thunder here…)

In 2037, a dinosaur is going to be discovered in North Dakota, after someone spots it munching on a deer in the middle of the forest. (HERE we go! Now, I can actually see this being potentially true. If you've never been out west, to the desert or the forest, you have NO IDEA how vast and uncharted parts of this country — and this world for that matter — actually are. I can totally see there being vestigial beings, whether they're ancient relatives to dinosaurs or bigfoot or whatever, still being around and so scarce that we hardly ever see them in civilization. And, I mean, really, at this point, can you blame them for wanting to avoid people? You think Bigfoot wants to be getting into fights with people on Facebook over memes?)

An Interdimensional War with aliens called the Nirons is going to start within the next decade, when the Russians fire upon one of their craft. (Thanks a lot, Putin. Jerk.)

I, Sean Leary, am going to become a multimillionaire, critically-acclaimed best-selling author this year. (I completely agree with this, time traveler.)

Anyway, I first wrote about ThatOneTimeTraveler back in October, when he/she/it began posting a number of predictions (one of which was claiming that Donald Trump was going to win the 2020 presidential election, so, ya know, grain of salt on the rest of this stuff.) I find stuff like this to be fascinating, and regardless of whether or not I believe it, I find it to be entertaining. At the very least, I admire the imagination of it, and it's a fun, escapist distraction.

And honestly, @thatonetimetraveler isn't the only person claiming to be a time traveler on TikTok, and they're not even the most popular person claiming to be a time traveler over the past couple of decades.

Probably the most famous person was John Titor, who came to prominence back in the '90s and '00s.

Back in those days, one of the most famous radio shows in the country was the Coast To Coast AM Show, hosted by Art Bell.

I used to work the night shift at the newspapers, and so every evening between midnight and 5 a.m. I would listen to Art, who was a fantastic character broadcasting from the middle of the Nevada desert. (Side note: On a cross-country drive, I decided to try to find Art's studio in Parumph, Nevada, and it really IS in the middle of freakin' nowhere.) Bell would host shows about UFOs and ghosts and werewolves and, of course, time travelers, which were one of his favorite topics.

In fact, Bell was so into the whole time travel idea that he would, from time to time (pun intended) open up a phone line specifically for time travelers.

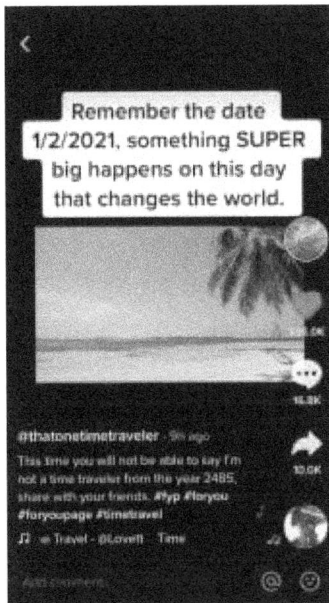

During many Bell shows, he dove into the stories of a mysterious character claiming his name was John Titor, which was actually a name thought to be short for "John TimeTraveler" that was used on several bulletin boards during 2000 and 2001 by a poster claiming to be an American military time traveler from 2036.

Titor made several incredible claims, including that he was here to help save the world from the Y2K bug, and that he was here to warn us about several calamities, including a nuclear war, mass famines, and Nickelback.

Of course, none of them came true (other than Nickelback), and evidence was later discovered that the whole Titor thing was probably an elaborate hoax. Probably by the manager of Nickelback.

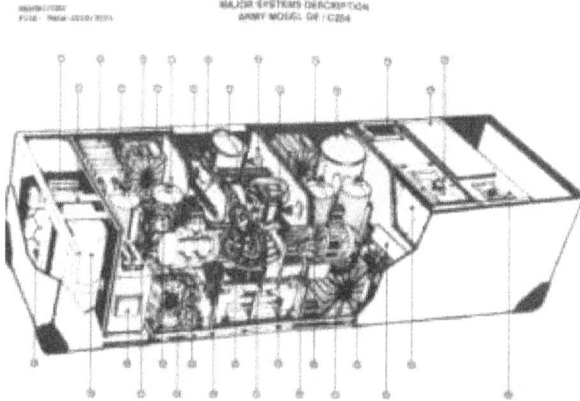

John Titor's alleged time travel device. Also makes toast and can chop onions like a charm!

In all likelihood, @thatonetimetraveler is probably doing the same thing. I mean, c'mon now, the manager of Nickelback probably has a lot of time on his hands.

But, honestly, who cares?

They're not really hurting anyone, other than people goofy enough to go overboard in taking them seriously (and let's face it, if you're taking a time traveler on TikTok seriously, you probably have far bigger issues to deal with) and at least the person is entertaining.

So, what do you think?

I guess we'll find out.

And as a time traveler myself, albeit one who only travels to the future one second at a time, I'm going to predict that THIS is what we're going to find out tomorrow...

Return To Earth, Alien David Bowie, And Save Us!

Jan. 8, 2021

In honor of David Bowie's birthday today, Jan. 8, Happy birthday, Bowie, whatever planet you're on…

Ever wonder what music made by an extraterrestrial might sound like?

Apparently, kind of like this:

"Let's dance

put on your red shoes

and dance the blues…"

Which, if you play it backwards, sounds like this:

"Dance let's

shoes red your on put

blues the dance and laser beam cattle rectums. . . "

Amazing how that works, isn't it? And you thought only Selena Gomez wrote about laser beaming cattle rectums, didn't you? Little did you know . . .

Anyway, of course, the song I'm talking about is "Let's Dance," by Alf.

Well, no, it's "Let's Dance," by the late legend David Bowie. (Alf sings that song that goes, "I'm in love with a stripper . . .") But there might not be much of a difference between Alf and David — aside from the need by one of them to buy shampoo in industrial-sized tubs. (Sorry Bowie, but your vanity must be exposed!)

According to a story from the summer issue of Paranoia Magazine, written by that breathtakingly trustworthy investigative reporter Anonymous, the dear departed Bowie may have been an alien being sent here to live among us earthlings. Or, he may have been abducted by aliens and entrusted with spreading their message to humans. Or, "Anonymous" may have spent a lot of time with our old friend Zuga the ganja farmer.

Regardless, the story makes for some interesting reading, and brings up some intriguing points.

Especially if by "intriguing points" you mean stuff that's complete and utter bat crap nuts but is nonetheless fascinating and amusing to contemplate.

The first bit of "evidence," naturally, goes back to Bowie's breakthrough LP, 1969's "Space Oddity." The cover features Bowie, an alien, and a spaceship. It's quite a love triangle. Sorry Bowie, but I don't like your chances. Alien and spaceship were meant to be together like chocolate and nougat.

But beyond that delicious thought, Anonymous wonders "…whether the inclusion of alien figures and spacecraft on the sleeve were supposed to indicate that aliens were working with Bowie…"

If they were, they managed his career well. (Maybe Justin Bieber should consider hiring them?) Because the more the alien motif popped up in Bowie's work, in such discs as "The Man Who Sold The World" and "The Rise And Fall Of Ziggy Stardust And The Spiders From Mars," the bigger Bowie got.

Art Bell: King of Late Night Media, Archduke of Lunatic Bullshit.

In 1976, David starred in "The Man Who Fell To Earth," as "Humpty Dumpty." Oh, sorry, my bad. Actually, he played a visitor from an alien world. (Grimace from McDonald's played Humpty Dumpty – and earned an Oscar nomination for his role. Because he's just that good. And fat. And purple.) Bowie's part in that critically-acclaimed film sparked the rock star's career as an actor.

Seven years later, he played a vampire in the movie "The Hunger," which was based on a book written by Ronald McDonald, about the new 20 piece McNuggets. Oh, wait, no, actually, it was written by Whitley Strieber, who rightfully told me not to use two McDonald's jokes in this column, but did I listen to him?

No. No, I did not.

Anyway, Strieber, who, come to think of it, sounds like a guy who wears a lot of plaid and works in an old-timey bicycle shop that fixes those bikes with one giant wheel on the front and one tiny one on the back, claims to have been abducted by aliens several times. Could these aliens have been the agents of David Bowie, pitching him for the role, giving Strieber "an offer he couldn't refuse?" I guess it's more extreme than the author waking up with a horse's head next to him, but maybe anal probes are the preferred hard-line negotiating ploy of the alien mafia?

Bowie further stoked the flames of speculation by releasing the single "Loving the Alien" in 1985. The video for "Loving" shows Bowie suffering a nosebleed — and as Anonymous points out, nosebleeds are typical symptoms of alien abductees. (Why? Because the tracking implants are embedded in their sinuses. Duh!!! And, also, because alien abductees love their cocaine.)

Anonymous continues that these various clues are just "the tip of the iceberg," which is also where he started to get these ideas (that's two cocaine jokes and two McDonald's jokes for those of you counting at home) and that "A great deal of evidence has been found in David Bowie's work which shows beyond any reasonable doubt that he has been influenced by aliens."

More evidence is apparently found in the hit song "Jean Genie."

Bowie has claimed the hit is about Iggy Pop. Nice try, buddy.

Anonymous cites the lyric "poor little greenie" as referencing little green men; the lyric "sits like a man but smiles like a reptile" as descriptive of a reptilian alien race often described in abduction scenarios; and the title itself as being a tip-off to its non-earthly subject.

After all, Anonymous writes, Chambers 20th Century Dictionary defines genie as "a class of spirits in Muslim mythology, formed of fire, living chiefly on the mountain of Kaf which encircles the world, assuming various shapes, sometimes as men of enormous size and porentious (sic) hideousness."

But enough about Rush Limbaugh.

Another incriminating line, Anonymous claims, is "talking 'bout Monroe and walking on Snow White," which may point to the fairy tale about dwarves (i.e. aliens), or, in all fairness, may tip to Iggy Pop babbling about a Marilyn fetish while snorting coke. (There's three coke references. Catch up, McDonald's!)

"He bites on a neon and sleeps in a capsule" and "the Jean Genie loves chimney stacks" are also allegedly subtle nods, for referencing both space capsules and Father Christmas — "who flies through the air like a UFO." Although in his case, the F could stand for fat. Like Grimace. (Three to three! Who's going to win??? The suspense is unbearable!)

"In conclusion," Anonymous writes, "it can be said that a significant portion of the lyrics to the song 'The Jean Genie' as well as the title itself have an unmistakable alien connotation. It seems to be almost impossible that David

21

Bowie could have written, for example, the line 'poor little greenie' without intentionally associating it with the phrase 'little green men'..."

(Insert booger joke here.)

Now, it seems strange, but Anonymous may be on to something. After all, Bowie later named one of his tours "Area 2," an obvious reference to the infamous Area 51 in the Nevada desert, a government base reputed to be a haven for extraterrestrial craft.

The co-headliners on the tour were Moby, who appears as a spaceman in his video for the song, "We Are All Made of Stars;" and Outkast, which released an album called "ATLiens" and which repeatedly references UFOs and E.T.s in their lyrics. Especially aliens that like ta "shake it like a Polaroid pict-cha!"

Last, but not least, a profile feature of Bowie and Moby in Entertainment Weekly boasted the headline "Loving the Aliens."

So, at this point, you're probably asking, "Can you pass me those Doritos?"

And you're probably also asking, "Sean, are you saying that you believe David Bowie was actually an alien? Do you think that after he passed away he went back to his home planet? Do you think he was secretly protecting the earth and if he returned he could help save it? And, again, can you please pass me those Doritos????"

Yes, I can. Just don't bogart those, Telegram Sam.

As for whether the late, great Bowie was indeed an extraterrestrial, I don't know Scully, but there's only one way to find out.

Check one of Bowie's backstage concert riders.

If it specifies that Mr. Bowie must be supplied with plenty of Reese's Pieces and "an escape bicycle in case of an emergency," well…

famour Astrologer Says To Expect A WILD Inauguration Week...

Jan. 17, 2021

Anyone else got a bad feeling about this?

Wednesday will mark the inauguration of Joe Biden as the 46th President of the United States, and all indications are that it's shaping up to be a wild week and strange start to Biden's administration — and it DEFINITELY will be, according to one notable Astrologer who has predicted the election win and other major events.

"There are multiple things going on on inauguration day that are worth discussing, however I said this before, I'm particularly concerned first about the 19th and then the night of inauguration day," says Maren Altman, a famous Astrologer who has detailed a number of recent events and their charts on her TikTok, @marenaltman.

Why? Because there are some foreboding signs in the stars.

"Can you please stop giggling every time I mention Uranus?"

"Looking at the chart of Washington DC on the 19th and 20th the Mars Uranus conjunction will go exact and on the 20th during the inauguration ceremony the moon will be at the exact degree, 29 Aries, that Mars was at when the

24

capital was infiltrated and all that went down," Maren says on her TikTok.

Yikes.

"Previously I did say that the ceremony looks sleepy (pun intended? ok, maybe not…) because the Moon is in the

Expect to see a lot of riots and unrest this week, and not just in Taylor Swift's love life! Whoh! HEL-lo! Thank you, thank you, please remember to tip your waitstaff…

12th, but I think that now, knowing that Mars was there when the riots took place, that there can be multiple overlays," Maren says. "For example, the ceremony is secluded and private and very safe, but there's ongoing riots and violence in other locations because later in the day, that night, 3-4 a.m. on the 21st, the Moon will cross Mars and Uranus, and I know Trump will not be at the inauguration. This is happening in his 10th house of publicity as well. So the 19th and the 20th is a critical time."

Trump's personal Astrology reading coincides with that, and given the alignment of the stars and planets, it's looks as if Trump will be launching a new career in a new media company. There are also signs that there's going to be a rocky spring and summer especially in regard to his relationship to the Republican party. Certainly plausible if he launches or partners with a competitor to Fox News, as he's talked about.

So, what about Biden's upcoming months?

"In looking at Biden's upcoming astrology for the next few months, inauguration day does look like one of the tensest times, like an unstable body or stressful period of Mars and Uranus and Taurus and the Moon joining it atop his moon

and water fortune, this looks like a pretty unstable and tumultuous period," Maren says. "However, with it happening on his lot of Fortune that's usually an indication of protection, so I think that this represents that yeah there's uprisings and riots and what not, but then he's protected because obviously inauguration day has massive security."

However, Biden will encounter unusual situations early on in his presidency, as his chart for late February and early March indicates, she says.

Not all will be bad for Joe, as the first two months beyond the inauguration strife look positive.

"There's going to be a focus on his living situation or family, like this could be a really private, dreamy situation, but it looks actually like... it's something with his family, a new beginning," she said.

However, in late March his chart indicates that he'll have "trouble with a known enemy or partner," which she interprets to potentially be clashes with Republicans possibly over covid or budget issues… or something completely bizarre.

Like Bigfoot? Bigfoot? Are we finally going to hear about the confirmation of the existence of Bigfoot????

"It's very weird, late March and early June are very weird," she says.

Like, BIGFOOT weird????

"Very weird."

Ok, be coy. I'll be waiting to see if it's Bigfoot.

That would be far more interesting than just more political fighting between the two parties. Unless the Republican party unveils their latest candidate to be Bigfoot. Man, imagine that. Imagine if the Republicans put Bigfoot up for election in 2024, and the Democrats put up the Abominable Snowman, and it was secretly revealed before the election that they were both Yetis, and part of the same Illuminati bloodline of Yetis…

Oh, sorry, I digress.

Back to the usual political B.S. fighting. Go figure, we're going to see more of that too, as both parties' signs indicate battling, as well as a transformation for both, Maren says.

@marenaltman

239	**1.0M**	**28.7M**
Following	Followers	Likes

Message   👤   📷   ▾

You can follow Maren Altman on TikTok for more Astrological interpretations.

"Even more so than the chart for the Democrats this year, the chart for the GOP shows it going through a dramatic rebirth," Maren says. "Coming out as a new image this spring and something even bigger towards the end of the year. This is a dramatic 'this is who we are dramatic rebranded identity.'"

She also predicts massive social unrest in May and June 2021, and the unearthing of many secrets and "things that have been hidden."

Ok. Interesting.

As for the coming decade, through 2032, there's going to be a massive reorganization of the financial aspect of the world, and the U.S. in particular. (Bitcoin, anyone?)

There's also likely to be wildfires and some food shortages in the summer, she says in addressing Nostradamus' predictions for 2021, and notes that there are a lot of astrological indications that the United States, and the world, are entering into a number of new beginnings.

Nothing about Bigfoot though. Oh well, we can check his chart. We know he's a Libra.

So, will Maren prove to be right? Hopefully if there are demonstrations, there's no violence and nobody gets hurt. We'll find out this week.

You can follow Maren on TikTok at @marenaltman, and check out her website as well for more insights.

Here's Who Joe Biden Desperately Needs To Help During His Presidency

Jan. 22, 2021

Like millions of other people, I watched the inauguration of Joe Biden as president this week, in part to see if Kanye West was going to jump on stage and claim that he should've won the award.

But as I was watching Joe talk about how he was going to help millions of Americans in need, to help them get the aid they so desperately seek, I couldn't help but think of one particular person I hope is rescued from her situation.

That person?

Taylor Swift.

Oh, no, wait, not her.

The person I'm talking about is, of course, Alice, the maid on "The Brady Bunch."

That's right.

Alice.

Recently, I spent a day laid up in bed, sick, with Gatorade and a TV remote as props to pass the time.

Flipping beyond the deluge of courtroom and self-help shows I found a real blast from the past.

"The Brady Bunch."

I didn't even realize old episodes of "The Brady Bunch" were still airing. When I was a kid, my siblings and I used to watch re-runs and make fun of them. But it's been a long time since I'd seen it on TV. I figured it had been superseded by shows like "Saved By The Bell," "Family Matters" and "Full House" on most programmers' schedules. But nope, there it was in all its strange, anachronistic glory.

There are so many goofy things about "The Brady Bunch" that it's impossible to list them all in such a limited space.

There are the bunk beds and the three-to-a-room setup, which was probably done so the show's producers only had to build two bedroom sets and the scriptwriters could hold important moments of dialogue between the kids in central locations.

(Yes, I know that's the cue to begin the deluge of e-mails from hardcore "Brady Bunch" fans telling me the REAL reason for the bedroom layout. I sit waiting to be corrected. And waiting to delete all your e-mails.)

There are the bizarre fashions. The anachronistic dialogue. The astro turf lawn. The economic implausibility of that many kids and a maid on an architect's salary.

Alice. She couldn't even afford a last name. Or a change of wardrobe, apparently.

And then there's the situation of Alice, the maid.

Keep in mind that Mrs. Brady doesn't work, so Alice is help for a stay-at-home mom whose kids are all in school. I guess if you're a highly-paid architect, as Mr. Brady obviously is — snicker, snort — you can afford that sort of thing.

But Alice goes beyond just being a maid. She's really kind of an odd, indentured servant.

For one thing, she's rarely seen out of her blue uniform and hardly ever seen doing anything but working. Night and day, weekdays and weekends, Alice is on the job. Don't the Bradys have to adhere to any labor laws?

Also, she lives at the house. In a shifty little area off the kitchen. What is this, medieval times, where the serfs work off their boarding on the lord's manor? Off-camera, does Mr. Brady parade around with a giant turkey leg in his hand, placing a pox on the house of Doug Simpson and beckoning "fyne wenche Alice" to fetch him a flagon of ale?

Being tied to the Brady stead means little-to-no privacy and little-to-no life for the poor woman. She's constantly on call. How many times have we seen Alice with some sort of mud mask on her face, a do-rag on her head, wrapped in her nightgown/high priestess robe, settling in for a well-earned night's rest, only to be yanked out of bed by some strange sound, Brady family emergency or phony UFO scare perpetrated by an unruly kid. It's really not fair.

Seriously, how did the Brady's fall into this situation? Did Alice lose a bet with Bobby and have to be the family's slave for life? Did they

Sam The Butcher. WAP magnet.

secretly purchase Alice as a mail-order bride for Sam the butcher to insure themselves fresh brisket for the remainder of their days? Or is she a communist spy, sent to infiltrate the residence in order to glean information on Mr. Brady's work for the government that allows him frequent access to the celebrities and astronauts that pop in for family visits?

I'm not quite sure.

But I am pretty sure about the strangest thing in regard to "The Brady Bunch": The fact that not only did it air on national TV, but that it was a huge hit. Think about it. At one point this show was the "Must-See TV" of its time. Millions of people set their evening schedules around watching it. And what's more, they took it seriously. It wasn't ironic or cheesy, it was the mainstream humor of its era to a significant segment of the audience.

Of course, 30 years or so on, that seems completely absurd.

It also makes you wonder, when you look around the current TV landscape, what shows will spur critics in 30 years to make the same bemused and bewildered observation.

One of my picks?

"The Bachelor."

Trust me, 30 years from now, people are going to be saying, "Ok, so these dozens of attractive women all had to go on this show and act like they were that desperate for male companionship? What, did they lose a bet? Was Sam the Butcher already taken?"

VanHyfte's Magical Creative World Lives On After His Passing

Jan. 29, 2021

From the time I first saw Tim VanHyfte's artwork, not long after I moved to the Quad-Cities in the mid-'90s, I was absolutely enthralled.

VanHyfte had a beautiful, intricate, original and wonderful style that was distinctly his own.

Most of Tim's subjects were women, and his artwork presented them as beautiful mysteries, fantastic worlds and journeys to be taken through merely the look in their eyes, the way they held themselves, the environments in which they were presented. It was reminiscent of a Gen X version of Andrew Wyeth's "Christina's World" — a striking image you couldn't help be pulled into and intrigued by.

VanHyfte passed away yesterday. He'd had some health complications, and then, a little more than a week ago, he got covid. The first few days were hopeful, and then things took a turn for the worst.

I knew him in a limited fashion — we weren't incredibly close friends, but were more like friendly acquaintances — but I greatly admired him as a creative person, and I still own two of his original artworks, as well as possibly his best known works, his album covers for Einstein's Sister.

That's actually how I knew him best, through my good friends Kerry Tucker and Bill Douglas from Einstein's.

Every time I saw Tim, he was incredibly friendly, amiable, and fun to talk to. We'd run into each other at various spots of interests — comic book shows, art galleries, Einstein's shows — and every exchange was laid back, friendly, and interesting. He was an intelligent and incredibly imaginative guy, with a broad palate of interests and talents.

VanHyfte had a number of gallery showings around the area, but his work got worldwide recognition on the cover of those four Einstein's Sister CDs, each of them a masterpiece in its own right. I remember seeing the first cover and being completely enthralled by it, and mentioning that in my review of the record, saying that it was "a welcome and perfect gateway to the brilliant sonic adventures within."

But VanHyfte was an artist's artist. He was always creating, whether in or out of the spotlight. One of his most notable and loved means of creative communication was through postcards he would randomly send to friends; miniature masterpieces that would arrive as keys to the world of his mind.

As Einstein's Sister lead singer and long-time VanHyfte friend Bill Douglas posted on his Facebook, "When someone asks you for your mailing address, you wonder what the heck is coming your way. When Tim VanHyfte did it, little did I realize then how I would be so fortunate as to receive these postcard-sized works of art every so often in the mail. He called it 'art therapy' for his creative soul, but to me, and I imagine so many others, it was a treasure to receive time and time again in a century that is losing touch with the simple act of sending physical cards and letters through postal delivery. I'm gonna miss this."

His friend Thomas Hernandez posted the following tribute:

"My Friend Tim VanHyfte died today.
I first met him in early September 1976.
In those 45 years he become as close as a brother to me.
The description we both landed on was he fell somewhere between a Family Doctor & Jiminy Cricket.
He was my friend and always stood by me.
My life was far richer and better for him being in it.
AND the world is a little bit darker and less interesting without him in it.
He was there with me when my son came into this world 2 and half months early. He was there when I got married. He was there when I got divorced.
We spent many countless hours just talking and laughing when I worked in Atkinson at the Convenience Store. I would give anything for just another of those hours.

He was an Artist. He was a writer. He was a comic & Sci Fi nerd and loved Star Trek. He loved History. He cared about the world around him. He was a deeply curious man who had a vast collection of books on every subject imaginable. I count myself fortunate to have some of his artwork.
He fiercely Loved his Family with all his heart.
He was there for every up and down in my life for the last 30 years.
I hope he knew how much he was valued in not just my life but in everyone's he touched.
I'll miss you my friend.
Vaya con Dios."
His friend, and my longtime friend, Toni Wilson posted,
"The loss of Tim was not just the loss of an artist — it was the loss of a friend and a father. This didn't need to happen. Godspeed, Tim. See you on the other side. Can't wait to see what kind of artwork you come up with over there!"
But our mutual friend Reid Robinson perhaps put it best in his post about Tim:
"Simply put,Tim VanHyfte was one of the kindest people I've ever known.
Rest well, brother."
Below are some of Tim's artworks, which, along with the lives he touched and the friendships he had, remain his legacy. A magical world which remains resonant in his wake.
Rest in peace, Tim.

Forget QAnon, Let's Recall The '90s Celebrity Who Admitted To Being Possessed By The Devil

Feb. 5, 2021

Between QAnon and the fashion return of flannel and ripped jeans, two of the hottest upcoming trends in pop culture seem to be '90s nostalgia and the belief in a bizarre conspiracy about celebrities secretly possessed by demons.

However, once upon a time, back in The Era of Cellphones The Size Of Bread Loaves, there was a celebrity who actually admitted that yes, he

"Hello, Egyptians? Was it really aliens who built the pyramids?"

was once possessed by demons, although he was also cured.

Odd? Odd, but true.

The Lord may work in mysterious ways, but the the way the devil works is obviously just plain strange. For example, God has been known to communicate to we humans through burning bushes, the angel Gabriel and his son, Jesus Christ. And beezlebub? Well, apparently, he's been sending us messages through the song "I Adore (Mi Amor)."

Yes, Bob Larson, an alleged exorcist, whose alleged exorcisms can be seen here, claims that one of the people he exorcised was Kevin Thornton — a singer with the group Color Me Badd.

I'm not kidding.

For those of you who don't remember which member was which in Color Me Badd (and that's likely most of you), Thornton isn't the lead singer with the bad facial hair who kind of looked like the devil — that is, if the devil used a lot of styling gel. Thornton is American guy with the dreads, the cheesy mustache and the flamboyant, "devil-made-me-wear-it" fashion sense.

Recently, on the radio show Coast To Coast AM, Larson talked about his encounter with Thornton, claiming that he didn't even know he was a singer in a band until he talked with "K.T." after the ministry shindig/demon-casting-out-soiree. After describing the event, Larson played a tape of the demon speaking through Thornton. The voice was cold and gutteral, and the wicked words it growled kind of sounded like this: "Tick-tock, you don't stop-stop, to my heart/Tick-tock, you don't stop-stop, to my heart/Oooo-oooh-oooh-oooh-oooh-oooh-oooh/I Wanna Seee-exx You Up…"

And you thought mumblerappers looked cool, check this ish out! Kickin' it old school!

Now, of course, I'm kidding. (Or AM I????) Seriously though, when I first heard this news, it was a real shock. Before, I just thought the "Badd" in Color Me Badd was a description of the group's music, but now, I guess it was supposed to mean bad in the evil sense. I'm assuming the second "d" was added as initialed props to the devil. And to think, some religious types only accused groups like KISS (Knights In Satan's Service), AC/DC (Against Christ/Destroy Christ) and Black Sabbath (Black Sabbath) of having wicked messages hidden in their names.

Other evidence of diabolical powers at work: Color Me Badd backwards is "Ddab 'em, Roloc!," which sounds like something very wrong that might happen in a Turkish bath house.

The b-side was "All 4 Stone Washing."

Of course, this could all be bogus. "K.T." could just be the victim of a hoax, or a co-conspirator in the perpetration of one. CMB hasn't exactly burned up the charts in about, oh, three decades. Maybe this is a publicity stunt, or maybe Kevin needed to pay some bills, so he took a job playing the part of a demon-possessed person so Larson could publicly "heal" him. After all, the source for all of this is highly dubious. Larson is a televangelist of the Benny Hinn persuasion, best known for his weekly Trinity Broadcasting TV show and his appearances on such revered and strenuously fact-checked daytime programs as "Montel" and "Sally Jesse Raphael."

During his time on Coast to Coast, and for days afterward, visitors to the message board ripped into Larson, calling him a charlatan at best and a grifter at worst. However, nobody really said anything about "K.T.'s" role in the whole enchilada.

So, I checked out the official Color Me Badd website, to see if, by chance, it could shed some light on the facts of the situation. I thought that maybe Thornton's bio would include an entry saying, "Kevin's career as a singer in Color Me Badd was cut tragically short when he was possessed by a gravelly-voiced demon in 1995. While the physical symptoms of the infestation gave his live performances a new energy — who could forget the time he spun his head around completely during an encore in Dallas! — his new, ragged vocal style left him unable to hit those high notes anymore. His former bandmates wish him all the best!"

Color Me Hungryy!

But nope. I do now know his favorite color is RED though, so maybe that's a hint? (Illuminati????!!!!????)

However, digging deeper, which we hard-hitting investigative reporters do when dealing with information this important, revealed that indeed Kevin had said he had battled "demons" and had turned to Jesus and away from his past.

Good for you, Kevin Thornton. You go, Glenn Coco!

However, I also found out that Thornton should probably offer an exorcist's business card to his fellow bandmate Bryan Abrams. Two years ago, bandmate Mark Calderon was hospitalized after being victim of an on-stage attack from Abrams, who was drunk and according to witnesses (and video) was screaming "I'm "I'm motherf—ing Color Me Badd!" after he shoved Calderon. Looking at his mug shot, Abrams probably should've been yelling "I'm fluffernuttering Color Me Type 2 Diabetes!" but, ya know, details.

All 4 Love indeed.

I offer Abrams, and his band members, my most sincere thoughts and prayers.

And, also, here's Bob Larson's phone number.

Time Travelers Reveal This Year's Super Bowl Winner, And It's...

Feb. 7, 2021

About half a football field's throw ago, I wrote a column about an alleged time traveler from the year 2485.

I wrote it as a joke, of course, because I can only take time travel so seriously. As a concept, I find it fascinating, as I find all esoteric science and the ilk fascinating, and of course time travel has been proven theoretically possible, so I don't completely discount it out of hand.

However, I also use a generous serving of salt grains when reading about alleged time travelers. And I add limes and tequila.

There are plenty of time travelers on TikTok, the social media platform that's usually dominated by girls in bikinis dancing, people doing stunts that look like they probably really really hurt, and various other goofy and funny videos. And of course there are plenty of time travelers picking the winner of today's Super Bowl, as if making a 50/50 bet is an incredible leap.

Tell me the final score and some of the highlights before the game, and I'll be convinced. Say that the Bucs are going to win and, well, meh.

Before I reveal the consensus of the Super Bowl winner, according to five different time travelers on TikTok — and the funny thing is, there is no unanimous consensus, three say one team and two say the other, so... different timelines?

But, honestly, who cares?

They're not really hurting anyone, other than people goofy enough to go overboard in taking them seriously (and let's face it, if you're taking a time traveler on TikTok seriously, you probably have far bigger issues to deal with) and at least the person is entertaining.

Now, before I reveal the Super Bowl pick of three of the five time travelers I surveyed on TikTok, let me say that I am not a financial advisor, nor am I a bookie or anyone recommending you put money on this pick, or anything else that might get people all pissed off at me. This is purely for entertainment purposes. Kind of like most of the halftime shows.

And like many of the post-game shows.

Which, according to three out of five time travelers, will be talking about the Chiefs winning their second consecutive Super Bowl.

Have fun, be safe, and have a great Sunday!

Three Out Of Five Time Travelers WRONG On Super Bowl

Feb. 7, 2021

When you can't trust a random person claiming to be a time traveler on TikTok, really, who CAN you trust?

Three out of five alleged time travelers on TikTok claimed that the Kansas City Chiefs were going to win the Super Bowl.

And, well, we saw what happened.

A romp of 31-9 for the Bucs.

Tom Brady dominated the Chiefs and cemented his GOAT status with another Super Bowl ring, disappointing the Kansas City fans, as well as the one or two people who actually believe folks claiming to be time travelers on TikTok.

Yes. It's a sad day when you can't trust random strangers claiming to be time travelers on TikTok.

But, hey, go Bucs!

Iowans Need To Ignore `Covid Kim' And Practice Covid Common Sense

Feb. 9, 2021

When you allow people with less intelligence and common sense to think for you and inform your decisions, the results are seldom good.

And that's why Iowans — and those traveling through Iowa in the Quad-Cities and throughout the state — need to ignore the abysmal advice of short-sighted Governor Kim Reynolds and trust scientists and their own common sense and good judgement in regard to covid.

"This virus ain't gonna spread itself!"

Memes have been flooding social media and the hashtag #CovidKim has been trending since Gov. Kim Reynolds decided to pull restrictions from Iowa.

Over 5,000 people have died in Iowa since the pandemic began, 60 percent of those in the last three months, according to the Iowa Department of Health.

Sixty percent. Over the last three months.

That's going back to November, when Reynolds finally started to pay attention to actual science and the fact that her state was becoming a national embarrassment and put forth a mitigation and shutdown order that was practical and hardly draconian. Many thought she didn't go far enough, in asking people to mask up, limit the number of people at public events, socially distance, and to impose hours and quarantine measures upon businesses, most notably bars, which have been shown to be some of the worst spots for the spread of covid, according to studies.

But on Friday, even as Iowa was trending, ONCE AGAIN, as one of the worst spots in the country for covid-19 safety, Reynolds decided to make the utterly moronic decision to pull back on all restrictions. And to make it worse, she did so right before Super Bowl Sunday, as health professionals across the country were warning that Super Bowl parties could turn into covid superspreader events and spike up cases.

This also came on the heels of Reynolds, even in her bubble of ignorance, surely being aware that the new, far more virulent strain of covid-19 was here in Iowa and starting to sink its claws in.

It's hardly surprising that the Associated Press reported on Monday that Reynolds didn't consult with scientists and health professionals before she decided to sentence hundreds and maybe thousands more Iowans to death with her asinine stupidity and pathetic lack of leadership.

And that is essentially what she's done.

Last week, more than a dozen friends of mine posted on social media about having caught covid, and two people I knew — a friend and a relative — died from it. Those two join over two dozen other people I've known — many of whom were well-known around the Quad-Cities arts and media scene — who have died from contracting it.

And the most infuriating and frustrating thing about it is that this entire thing, this entire pandemic, didn't have to be this bad.

The covid situation has been handled horribly from the start by a cadre of idiots, opportunists, and bubble-headed conspiracy nuts in positions of power who have ignored science and the advice of experts and put the safety of the public at risk through their selfishness and stupidity. Kim Reynolds is one of them. Aside from a few exceptions, she's largely been on the wrong side of history and science in regard to the pandemic, which is a complete abdication of her responsibility to represent the best interests of her constituents.

And that includes businesses.

There's been an artificial divide created among businesses and the public throughout this pandemic that's been nefarious and insidious, as well as contrary to good sense and judgement. The faster the pandemic is under control, the better it is for businesses in the big picture. Ergo, the more decisive and smart the decisions made by politicians to control it, the better. Certainly, businesses and employees were going to take a hit. That was inescapable and out of anyone's control at the onset of the pandemic. But it's been the mishandling of the pandemic and

Iowa Governor Kim Reynolds

response to it which has made things worse for the business sector by unnecessarily drawing it out longer than it needed to be, not to mention politicians being stingy and craven in their lack of substantive support for many small businesses.

However, as I mentioned, this didn't have to happen. This didn't have to be this difficult.

Scientists and health professionals, from the start, have advocated simple, common sense measures in regard to slowing the spread and ameliorating the damage and death from it.

Wear a mask.

Practice social distancing.

Wash your hands.

Keep your immune system up — take multivitamins, take vitamin D, take vitamin C, watch your diet and keep good habits.

52

None of these are difficult. None of them are anything more than common sense. They're all incredibly simple to do.

And yet when people in positions of power and authority don't do them, don't advocate them, and at worse diminish them and the threat of the pandemic, the large number of followers in our population take their cue and do nothing and make things worse. That's why it's so imperative for them to set a good example and make good decisions.

There are certainly cases to be made for adjusting tactics in the face of changing information. As more data came in about outdoor activities not being as virulent in regard to the spread of the virus, it would've made sense to allow some outdoor sporting activities and other outdoor events. And conversely, as some locations and events became all the more apparent as much higher risk areas for spread — such as bars — it made sense to curtail hours and enact policies to stop the spread. A comprehensive leadership plan would've also planned for the lost wages and profits inherent to such moves, and put in place plans to help those negatively impacted. That's what's been needed here all along, and despite it being blatantly obvious, it's been sorely lacking.

On a local and state level, there are ways in which real leaders could make an impact. Go on facts and fact-based data. Listen to healthcare professionals and scientists who are experts in the field. Follow their recommendations. Make your decisions accordingly.

In far too many instances, Kim Reynolds has not only not done so, she's moved in the opposite direction of all logic and common sense, and data shows that she's made things worse.

That's not based on wanton negativity, it's based on data, facts and extrapolation of both.

Covid numbers throughout the United States are insane and we as a country have just become numb to them to dull the impact.

Among the top 10 days marking the one-day greatest losses of life in the history of this country, the majority of them are deaths due to covid.

During November, Iowa was named as the worst state in the country for covid, with Cedar Rapids the worst city in the entire U.S. and Iowa holding several of the spots in the top 20 hot spots.

Since Iowa and Illinois went to mitigation measures, Iowa on Nov. 17, and Illinois on Nov. 20, the numbers in both states have slowly sloped downwards.

But that hasn't changed the fact that Iowa's number of infections has been consistently three times or more larger than Illinois' number, despite Illinois having roughly four times the population of Iowa.

The death tolls are usually roughly the same in terms of daily numbers, which, again, does not look well for Iowa given that their population number is far lower than Illinois and their population density is nowhere near as high.

People certainly gave Illinois Governor J.B. Pritzker plenty of blame and grief for putting Illinois under much more restrictive measures. But it worked.

Illinois Governor JB Pritzker at his press conference today.

Illinois' numbers have been greatly reduced. Like many countries around the world, Illinois has been able to more safely cut back on mitigations because they took the step of putting those stronger restrictions in place, and so, Pritzker's move to cut back on restrictions makes sense, based on the falling numbers. But even in the midst of pulling back on the restrictions, Illinois is still encouraging simple, common-sense measures like masks and social distancing.

Reynolds' decision shows none of Pritzker's leadership, intelligence, or relation to science and data. It's a rash and petulant action in contradiction to her own health experts' recommendations being done seemingly for political reasons, despite the fact that the virus infects and kills folks regardless of their political parties — a fact that, sadly, Reynolds is likely once more going to discover.

However, Iowans don't have to become victims to the stupidity of covid Kim.

Ignore her, and think for yourselves. Use common sense. Wear masks. Wash your hands. Keep your immune system up. Be smart about the activities you engage in. In lieu of any actual leadership on the part of the governor, you're going to have to do this yourself.

As I mentioned at the onset of this column, when you allow people with less intelligence and common sense to think for you and inform your decisions, the results are seldom good.

It's time for intelligent Iowans to show Kim Reynolds what common sense looks like, and, in doing so, show her what real leadership looks like, as well.

Iowans Are Smarter Than 'Covid Kim,' And They're Proving It

Feb. 10, 2021

Yesterday, I wrote about the moronic decision by Iowa Governor Kim Reynolds to do away with her already minimal efforts to mitigate covid-19 — just as statistics were showing that Iowa is one of the worst, and least safe, states in the country in regard to keeping its citizens covid-free.

I'd say her actions were ill-advised, but apparently, Reynolds took no advice in regard to making them. She ignored scientists, healthcare professionals (you know, those people she loves to pose for photo ops with, and hollowly praise as "heroes" while undercutting them with her actions) and any reasonable advisors, all of whom would've told her to keep the mitigations in place, or augment them, especially since Iowa was going into a dangerous period, with the new, more virulent strain of covid being found in the state.

Thankfully, an informal survey of me driving around to more than three dozen area businesses today, and looking over various Iowa businesses' social media pages, displays a glaring fact that's both inspiring and pathetic.

Highest Death Rate

47. Tennessee

48. Arizona

49. Iowa

50. South Carolina

51. Alabama

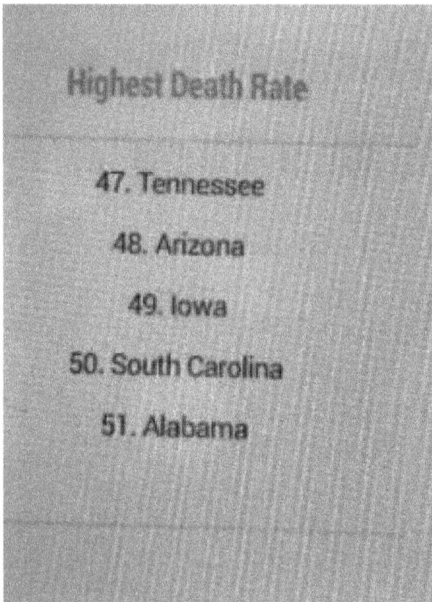

Iowa is 49th (next to last) in highest death rate from covid-19. (The data also included Washington D.C., which is not yet an official state, hence the 51 list.)

People are almost entirely ignoring Kim Reynolds and her stupid decision.

Every single place I've gone to today — and this is completely anecdotal and shouldn't be taken as a scientific study, merely an extrapolation of personal experience — is still requiring masks, is still practicing some form of social distancing and precautionary modifications to ameliorate any risk to customers and patrons.

From restaurants to automotive repair spots to big box stores to smaller local businesses, everywhere I went continued to ask for patrons to be masked. Everywhere I went had some form of modification to accommodate and consider covid-19 and to help protect patrons.

And on social media, businesses from The Book Rack to the German American Heritage Center and more have posted that they will continue to engage in safe practices in consideration of their patrons.

It's inspiring in many ways to see people behave in a smart, considerate and responsible manner. And quite frankly, when you look at what they're asking, it's really not much.

"This virus ain't gonna spread itself!"

Memes have been flooding social media and the hashtag #CovidKim has been trending since Gov. Kim Reynolds decided to pull restrictions from Iowa.

Wear a mask.

Social distance.

Use hand sanitizer provided by the businesses.

Be smart.

And yet when you look at how rather simple those instructions are, when you consider they're really a relatively minor inconvenience, it puts Reynolds' gutless and brainless actions into more sharper relief.

It also makes you wonder who Reynolds is actually representing, and whose interests she's serving, because it certainly doesn't seem to be those of the citizens of Iowa.

Iowans deserve better than Kim Reynolds.

Because Iowans are better than Kim Reynolds.

Politicians need to start remembering that when they're elected they cease being only politicians — people playing political games — and that they, through the result of that vote, become representatives. That is, they've been elected, they've been given a job, to REPRESENT their

constituents. They are there, they have been hired through the democratic process, to REPRESENT the best interests of the constituents.

In their position, they are given the advantage of a far wider array of tools and informational avenues than the vast majority of those constituents. It is their responsibility to best utilize those advantages. Read the information.

Consider it. Make the best decisions for your public, the people you represent, based upon that.

Kim Reynolds has not done that in this case.

And this case is a pretty big one.

Kim Reynolds has abdicated her responsibility and not done her job, and in this case, her incompetence could literally be a case of life or death.

Thankfully, Iowans are much smarter than Kim Reynolds.

Thankfully, Iowans are much more responsible than Kim Reynolds.

It's heartening and inspiring to see, and I commend Iowa businesses and Iowans for caring enough for their fellow citizens to engage in considerate and responsible action.

It's sad the person elected to ostensibly represent them isn't on their same level.

One hopes that when it's time to vote for governor next time, Iowans remember this, and regardless of political party, they elect someone who represents them, and their interests, much better.

"Why Do You Write About Covid So Much?"

Feb. 11, 2021

Imagine someone you love.

Someone who truly has impacted your life.

Someone you can't imagine life without.

Now imagine life without them.

Imagine how devastated you would be, how drowned in sadness you would feel.

I see people expressing this feeling every day on social media.

People who have lost loved ones to covid.

Their posts are heartbreaking. They exude sorrow and helplessness, as they struggle against the fact that someone who meant so much to them, who was so much a part of their world, is now gone.

Many of these people are older. Many are parents, who were the foundation to their children's lives, who were always there for them, who loved them unconditionally. Many more are grandparents, who taught their children and grandchildren, who were the ones who watched them and guided them and left them with incredible memories that shaped the people they are now.

It's incredibly sad to see people post about the losses of these people.

It's incredibly sad for me to have lost people who are family and friends, people who meant something to me, who live on in memories, but who I'd much rather have as a part of my life.

Someone messaged me yesterday, asking me why I write about covid so much. Why don't I just stick to entertainment writing?

People have said to me, why do you make such a big deal about it?

Many of those people haven't lost anyone close to them. Yet.

And it's sad that some people have to experience that loss for themselves to really get it, to suddenly recognize that this is real, that this is something that's more than just an eye roll or a political game or something to post about on social media as you make fun of people for wearing masks as if you're so much more rugged and tough for not wearing one.

It takes a stronger person to feel compassion for others. It takes a stronger person to feel empathy for others. It takes a stronger person to look at someone else's pain and not only feel sorry for them, but to recognize that they're part of a greater humanity, and that if you can take an action, especially one that's so relatively small, to prevent others from feeling that pain, to prevent others from losing their lives, then you should be strong enough to take that action, to make that small sacrifice because in some way, it may help someone's life be better, it may help save someone's life.

This is why I write about covid so much.

I didn't intend to. When this pandemic started, my reporting was still confined to entertainment and features, positive news. Then it transitioned to news about places closing down, events being canceled, the ways in which the entertainment world was changing.

Then it was about how the arts and entertainment world was pretty much shut down, as millions of people nationwide were left without jobs, without careers, without livelihoods.

Then, sadly, I started to have to write obituaries, as people I knew, as people who had been a part of countless people's lives on the local arts scene, began to fade away.

And as I was writing these stories, I started to notice, more, the ignorance and callousness of many people.

"Why should I change my life?"

"I'm not wearing no mask!"

"What are you, a covid freak?"

I have over 15,000 people across all my social media platforms, so I see a lot, I get a pretty good cross-section of humanity as I look over them. And what I've seen has been disturbing to say the least. Even as people were dying, being hit hard by illness, losing their jobs and careers, their businesses, people continued to politicize something that above all should've transcended politics. A virus. A disease. A sickness. Something for which there were none of the artificial borders and tribalisms society inflicts upon us, to divide us and make us forget that we have far more in common than we have in differences.

People arguing, acting as if verifiable facts and data were somehow subject to the same dismissal and veracity as baseless opinion and conjecture, ridiculous conspiracy theory. And then some media outlets actually having the gall to publish absolutely moronic theories on things like 5G towers being somehow responsible for the illnesses as if the scientifically-proven existence of a virus was somehow being covered up by millions of doctors, nurses and scientists worldwide.

That's why I started writing about covid. That's why I made sure to include links to all data points in my stories. That's why I made sure that all my reporting was FACT-based. So that people could have accurate and timely information without any spin, without any bias other than the bias towards giving people information and helping them live better lives, helping them save lives.

That's what I'm continuing to do.

Presenting accurate and fact-based information.

Asking people to take the very reasonable precautions of wearing masks, limiting social interactions, social distancing, having a good diet and exercise routine, taking vitamins like C and D as well as multivitamins and minerals to help boost your immune system. Common sense precautions. That's all I'm doing myself, that's all I would recommend people would do as well. Because THAT'S WHAT THE SCIENTISTS, HEALTHCARE

WORKERS AND EXPERTS ARE ADVISING US TO DO.

It's amazing to me that people will listen to experts and doctors in regard to so many things, and yet not this.

It's amazing to me that people will act as if the very simple, common sense advise of wearing a mask, social distancing, and boosting their immune systems, are such arduous chores.

It's amazing to me that people will look at the pain of others being ripped open on social media, and add their perfunctory "so sorry for your loss" comment without taking action to prevent others from suffering the same loss, even themselves.

I don't want to suffer those losses.

I don't want you to suffer those losses.

I don't care about your politics, your religion, what tribe you identify as.

I want us all to get through this, alive and well.

And that, that is why I continue to write about covid.

Remember This If You're Alone On Valentine's Day...

Feb. 12, 2021

"Do you feel as depressed as I do about being single on Valentine's Day?"

A friend of mine messaged me this question the other day, and it got me thinking, "Am I depressed at all about being single this Valentine's Day?"

And it got me answering myself rather quickly, "No. No, I am not depressed at all about being single this Valentine's Day."

Not in the least.

That's not to say that I'm a cold, heartless bastard with no sense of romance or desire for romantic love or a significant other in my life.

But it is to say that, this year, that's not a part of my existence, so, who cares?

I've had plenty of Valentine's Days during which I've been dating someone or in a relationship, or just in a casual fling with someone, and some of those still remain good memories.

Some do not.

But most of them do, and that's the way life goes.

Not everything is going to be fantastic 100 percent of the time. Sometimes things really sorta suck, and that's just the way it goes. You can't control other people and the way they feel, or, in some cases, the way they treat you, and the sooner you let go of the impulse to try to control others, the happier and lighter your life will be.

It's the same concept behind dating and meeting other people, whether in the real world or, as is more usually the case nowadays, online.

A woman friend of mine was talking to me recently and asked me about a guy who had randomly ghosted her on a dating app. She sent me a screenshot of the conversation, as well as a couple other convos with other guys, who had also ghosted her, and wanted to get a man's opinion on why she got ghosted and keeps getting ghosted.

(For those unfamiliar with the term, ghosting is when someone just stops messaging you back without any warning, goodbye, or sign off or indication whatsoever. They just… stop writing…)

After I had stated that I can in no way speak for all men, and that as a human being in general I'm such an outlier in the way I think and behave that it didn't surprise me in the least when a psychic once told me I was a space alien in human disguise, I told her not to bother worrying about it. Nothing in her conversations was "off putting" or intimidating in the least. They were just having random conversations and the guy split.

If you see this guy approaching you on Valentine's Day, it's not a good thing.

Yes, it is rude.

Yes, it is lame.

But, it happens.

To everyone.

For one thing, if a guy was going to do that, he wasn't worth her time or any of her concern. And for another, that's just the way most people are these days. That is to say, most people are spineless, capricious, morons with the communication skills and attention spans of crack-addicted chimps.

I also shared with her some of the famous, horrible, terrible last lines I wrote to women that caused them to ghost me on dating apps:

"So, did you see the new Bill and Ted movie?"

"That's cool. What led you to get into that as a career?"

"Lol. Yeah, no joke, 2020 has been the worst."

Controversial, I know.

If you see this guy approaching you, it's a far, far, worse thing.

Folks, to quote the Mandalorian, THIS IS THE WAY.

This is the way people are right now. I don't know what led to people being this strange, weak, and rude, but, they are.

So it's best not to really think too much about it. If someone ghosts you, THEY ARE A SPINELESS, INCONSIDERATE WUSS AND YOU ARE BETTER

OFF WITHOUT THEM. Move on. We live in a world of eight billion people, there are plenty of others out there. Some of whom, believe it or not, are not spineless, inconsiderate wusses.

I know, that is hard to believe.

But, trust me, the odds have got to be in our favor. Right, Katniss?

So, no, I'm not going to sweat it.

Just like I'm not sweating being alone on Valentine's Day. Because you know what? Being alone or just being with your friends or your kids really isn't so bad.

In fact, it's often preferable to being with someone, especially if they're a pain in the ass.

Take a look at your Facebook feed, and look at all the "happy relationships" out there. And while you're at it, look at Instagram and take a drink for every person you see posting some saccharine sweet thing about their relationship when you know for a fact one or both of them are cheating on the other.

It's why I've been sans relationship, and just dating, keeping things light, for so long. I'm honest and up front about my intentions and expectations and remain so throughout to avoid any miscommunication or misunderstanding. You know, like an adult should be. If someone isn't interested, ok, cool, adios and I wish you the best. Lots of single fish in an ocean of eight billion.

Moving on...

And I like the freedom. I do what I want, when I want, and take along the companions I want. If someone wants to come along for the ride and have some fun, cool. If not, that's cool too.

If you're really looking for something romantic to give your honey, here's the thing to totally get you laid.

You do what what you want to do, I'll do the same. I'm like Doctor Who, I travel through time one day at a time, pop up in different scenarios, take along companions for a while, we have some adventures, then we part ways amicably.

It's really not such a bad way to be. In fact, it's quite good. And so, this Valentine's Day, I'll probably do as I've always done over the past 13 years if I've been single, and I'll get a heart-shaped pizza and some Whitey's with my son, and hang out with him and play soccer and video games and jenga and watch "The Last Dance" or "The Mandalorian" or "Cobra Kai" for the umpteenth time with him.

And it'll be awesome. It'll be fun.

There she is hiding in my bushes and looking in my window again. Sigh. Ok, fine, I guess I'll go out with you, Olivia Munn...

Because when it comes down to it, the day is about love. It's about being with who you love. Celebrating that love, whether romantic or otherwise. And it's about being happy. So, do something for the people in your life who you love — and that should include yourself.

Have fun. Be happy. Celebrate the love you have in your life, regardless of who it's with — significant other, friends, family, or whoever.

And remember one very important thing.

All those chocolates you see on those store shelves…
…are going to be very deeply discounted over the next week.

And they taste just as good, whether they're heart shaped or not, so, enjoy that s**t.

Happy Valentine's Day!

Morgan Wallen And Gina Carano Stories Highlight Volcanic Divides In Our Society

Feb. 13, 2021

So, a country music star, Morgan Wallen, is caught on tape using the N word, which is not acceptable.

His record company, radio stations, etc. express condemnation of it. Right thing to do.

He admits his mistake and is contrite about it, does all the right things under the circumstances and seems sincere. Again, right thing to do.

And then...

wait for it...

wait for it...

His record sales SKYROCKET.

Now, do I think that suddenly racists were like, "You know what? I need something to listen to in the car, other than Gavin McInnes, so how about that country music guy who just made a racist slur?"

Well, yeah.

I'm sure certainly there were people who saw that as a dog whistle, regardless of the musician's apology, and flew to support him purely out of hatred and spite.

But in addition to that I'm also certain there were a lot of dipshits who wanted to support him just to "own the libs."

Morgan Wallen. I didn't have any idea who this guy was until this week. Because he's not a member of an obscure British indie band or a TikTok rapper.

And, folks, this is the knee-jerk binary polarity we live in.

If you're disliked by one side, the other side automatically likes you, and if you're pilloried and hated by one side, the other side automatically LOVES you.

This despite the fact that those same people would never defend certain actions if they were being done by a member of their opposite tribe, and in fact would absolutely revile them if they were the wrong star-bellied sneech.

It's crazy.

We're seeing the same thing play out with the Gina Carano story.

Now, from the information I currently have, it seems Carano is a different case in terms of context and repeated offensive statements. There haven't been a lot of other Morgan Wallen moments of racism or stupidity being reported. Could be out there, don't know, they don't pop up immediately in a web search.

Unlike with Carano.

When I first began writing this column, I did not know the depth of what the former "Mandalorian" star said or posted. I was not deeply educated on the social media writings of Gina Carano. Nor, quite frankly, did I want to be. I have better things to do with my life.

I saw one of her posts quoted in a story, which was just a really bad comparison of conservatives feeling sorry for themselves to Jews being literally prosecuted in Nazi Germany. Bad comparison? Yes. Insensitve? Yes. Virulently anti-semitic? Debatable.

Then I saw the picture that accompanied her tweet, which was not in the story I originally saw, and which I will not include here, of a half-naked woman in graphic distress being chased down the street, hunted down. That's a terrible analogy and an awful image to include needlessly in regard to your facile and whiny stretch of an argument.

And then I did a deep dive into some of her other posts, and I amend my statement with the caveat that now I wish I was not deeply educated

Now, Morgan Wallen needs to apologize for this shirt. No apology needed for the mullet and mustache combo.

on the social media postings of Gina Carano.

Carano's Twitter feed is a greatest hits cesspool of conspiracy bullshit and tired bigotry, a ditto of so much other bullshit out there on social media.

And although I do agree with her that Jeffrey Epstein didn't kill himself, a lot of the rest of the stuff is pretty damn moronic and small-minded, and, yes, insensitive to Jewish people in comparing her whining about people challenging her speech to Jews literally being hunted and killed in Nazi Germany.

Is she anti-semitic? I don't know. I didn't do THAT deep of a dive into her Tweets to see anything that was more anti-semitic than clueless and a bad analogy, but, that's been the claim.

Which is very interesting because here we have someone who was fired from her job at Disney for allegedly repeatedly posting anti-semitic material and commentary...

...who is now hired by a company run by a very publicly open orthodox Jewish man, Ben Shapiro.

So either what she said did not offend Shapiro, or Shapiro wants to own the libs so bad that he's fine letting it go. (Unlike his alleged fetish for AOC's shoes...)

Just wait until you see what she posted about Chewbacca.

So, here we are. A massive portion of the population can't think for themselves and lets their tribe do that for them. A massive portion of the population ignores facts and evidence placed right in front of them which they would condemn if it were being done by the other side, but which they excuse and condone because it's being done by theirs.

Few people can just look at events outside of a filter and make a judgement call on them as being good or bad without considering the political alignment of those doing them.

Few people can look at this opinion I'm writing without feeling one way or another because they're so brainwashed to one side or the other.

This is why I belong to no political party.

This is why I don't like belonging to ANY groups or organizations.

Because I like making up my own mind. I like seeking out facts and evidence.

And I recognize that we're all human, we all make mistakes, we all do dumb or ignorant things sometimes, and I would rather consider people on the content of their character and their actions rather than automatically condemning or defending them because of their label.

OCASIO-CORTEZ'S CAMPAIGN SHOES TO BE FEATURED IN MUSEUM EXHIBIT
TheStory@foxnews.com

Ben Shapiro: "Swipe RIGHT!"

Listen, I have no problem with people agreeing or disagreeing with me. That's life. As I've mentioned countless times before, we should all beevolving human beings, myself included. I change and evolve all the time, adjusting my thoughts and opinions based upon new information and consideration of fact. That's why one of the people I've disagreed with most in my life is me, in the past, because I've changed my opinions on a myriad of issues and topics as I've learned new things and grown and evolved.

And we should ALL be like that.

Something new happens, you learn something different, you should change your thinking and feeling to adjust to that. And you should employ perspective upon it and not knee-jerk react tilting far to one side or the other where your only emotions are hate or love.

Life is not binary.

Everyone makes mistakes, including me, including you.

Including Morgan Wallen.

Including Gina Carano.

Morgan Wallen recognized that what he said was inappropriate, and he changed his behavior. If people are buying his records because of his ability to change, great. If they're buying his records because they support what he said, that's pretty damning and pathetic. But not to Morgan Wallen, to those who are buying the records because they support the use of the racial slur.

As for Gina Carano, she doubled down and played the victim and didn't grow and evolve from the experience, and is the poorer for it as a person by having people surrounding her who just support and buttress her ignorance.

Not even Boner would buy a ticket.

It's also very strange to me that she's now being supported and championed by a public figure who is very open about his staunch Jewish faith. It's very weird to me that the political desire to dunk on the libs would overshadow condemnation of anti-Jewish statements when you are faithfully Jewish. But I can't see into Ben Shapiro's mind.

Strange times we live in. And at the end of this column, I have no solutions. Only a statement: Our society has got to break out of this unthinking slavish devotion to their dual tribes. They have got to stop using freedom as a buzzword and start actually acting free — free to think for themselves.

And what I think for myself is that based on past history of similar projects, this new Gina Carano movie is probably really going to suck. And it'll probably co-star Kirk Cameron.

If You're A Human Being Living On Earth, You Need To Read This

Feb. 19, 2021

Welcome to the column for all carbon-based life-forms.

If you breathe oxygen, this is for you.

And if you live on a planet, especially Earth, well, then, you've come to the right place.

Sorry, but I'm just following the new trend in advertising: casting as absurdly wide a net as possible.

Products used to be advertised to a fairly specialized base. Each ad could be counted on to pander in its own unique way.

You'd have your commercials aimed at seniors, in which someone sincere who was on TV when it was still seen only in black-and-white would give a testimonial about the product.

Said commercial would end with the person looking into the camera and intoning something to the effect of, "And you know why I, Wilford Brimley, recommend Aunt Bea's Fiberrific Oatmeal? (Dramatic pause.) Because I eat it, too."

Then there were the opposite extremes — the ads aimed at kids and adolescents. You'd get loud music; quick cuts; scenes of people skateboarding off the rails at the Grand Canyon; some cute, acne-free twentysomethings posing as teens; and a voice-over guy yelling the merits of NEW! EXTREME! INSAAAAAAAANE! CHEET-OS!

Somewhere in between, you had ads aimed at guys (which usually featured attractive women, or athletes giving a testimonial) and ads aimed at women (which usually featured attractive athletes, or women giving a testimonial).

But somewhere along the way, marketers, in their zeal to lure customers, started to get increasingly desperate — and vague.

One automobile company markets its SUV/minivan/whatever it's calling its human transport right now as "the car for life." The car for life — because so many other cars are made for zombies, vampires, ghosts or the traditionally dead. I think most cars, aside from the hearse, are made for life, but maybe that's just me.

Then there's "the TV for men and women." I'm really glad they finally made one of those. I'd grown tired of having to share the tube with my dogs, who tend to want to watch "Lassie" and Animal Planet over and over.

And those electronics companies were so arrogant about ignoring humans. Heck, RCA even blatantly rubbed it in our faces by making sets that were tailored to specific canines — Jack Russell terriers — and then to completely chap us, it put two of the condescending mutts in its logo.

But it's not just big-ticket items getting the universal-net treatment.

I kid you not, this is a direct quote from the Colon Cleanse infomercial playing on late-night TV these days: "Anyone who has an intestinal tract, AND anyone who eats, needs to watch this!" Now THAT'S called targeting a very specific market. Boy, there are demographers out there who are seething with envy after hearing that.

But there are always loopholes, and the hard-hitting questioners in the crowd of an infomercial can consistently be counted on to find them. I can imagine the exchange...

Audience member: "Uhhh, yeah, uhhh, I have an intestinal tract, but I don't eat. I manufacture nourishment through photosynthesis. Is Colon Cleanse still for me?"

Program shill: "Of course. Half-man, half-vegetable swamp things ALSO need to be detoxified on a regular basis."

Cue star soaring across the screen, trailing NBC Peacock rainbow bearing the slogan "The More You Know ..." Although in that case, perhaps the less you know, the better.

So, if you'll excuse me, I'm going to end this column for all readers.

After all, I have two jealous dogs to taunt and zombie hitchhikers to avoid.

Serving Up A Column For People Hungry For Secret Information On Celebrities' Lives

Feb. 26, 2021

What did you have for breakfast this morning?

Orange juice? Me, too!

Coffee? Me, too!

Leftover pizza? Me, too!

I guess there must be some special bond between us. Something unique. Something real.

You know, I haven't felt this way since I read that Charlize Theron likes to drink Red Bull — just as I do. I hadn't felt that way since I had read that Sarah Michelle Gellar is a big fan of tiramisu — just as I am. Those revelations were important to me, my sense of identity and my sense of well-being because they gave me a tangible, iron-clad link to someone famous. And that, we all know, is the key to true self-worth.

So, I guess what I'm saying is, thank you, Entertainment Weekly.

But it's not just EW that deserves my gratitude. I read a lot of entertainment writing. Tons of magazines, books, websites, blogs — you name it. So I see a lot of the same phrases and conventions over and over.

One example: If the writers of celebrity profiles meet a star over a meal, and they typically do, they always describe what the person is eating, as if it's an incredibly pertinent detail. "Brad Pitt orders his ostrich-egg omelet with baby capers, prepubescent squid ink and just a touch of middle-aged cilantro …"

Why would anyone care what Brad Pitt, or any other celebrity, eats? Really, unless they're scarfing something incredibly weird, exotic, or illegal — heroin-and-spotted-owl quesadilla, anyone? — who gives a gosh darn about it? Or even a golly-gee willikers about it?

Does it really make you feel closer to a person if you know what he or she eats? Honestly? Does it surprise anyone? It's as if there's some intrinsic news value in the fact that celebrities eat food. As if everyone thought that once they became famous, they were suddenly able to get their nourishment solely from wearing Kabbalah bracelets.

All legal and illegal stimulants aside, they do have to eat to live. Still, they must not eat very often, because when they do it during an interview, they're not very demur about it.

In stories, celebrities are always described as "digging into," "tearing into" or "ripping into" their food, as if they're velociraptors devouring the fat D-list actor who gets bumped off first in "Jurassic Park 562." Now, if they actually did leap onto their chairs, squat on their haunches, bare-hand the greasy food, and attack it before throwing it, still warm, into their mouths, that would be one thing. But, with the possible exception of one of the Kardashians, I'm guessing they don't.

Some lame-o writers might say that they're using food as a metaphor for a celebrity's zeal for life or whatever project he or she is working on. Right. Some might say they're really trying to capture every detail of a story, although I never see those same writers go so far as to tell me what a celebrity smells like. Other writers might admit that they put those cliches in to either break up dialogue or, more likely, to slyly boast about actually having a meal with a major star.

Personally, I'd prefer to see the space devoted to something more important. Such as news about the subject's latest project; in-depth analysis of the star's creative process; or titillating, lascivious details on other famous people this star has slept with.
But hey, that's just me. The guy who had orange juice, coffee and leftover pizza for breakfast — just as Demi Lovato and Hugh Jackman did.

Rock Island Should Go Back To 3 a.m. Closing for Downtown

March 1, 2021

Imagine it's Super Bowl Sunday, pre-covid. You're in your home, minding your own business, watching TV, having a couple beverages with a number of friends, having a good time.

Across the street, you see lights on in your neighbors' houses. You see cars out front. They have guests too, and all of you are enjoying a weekend night.

Suddenly, the evening is split by the flashing lights and squeal of two police cars, and an ambulance in tow, roaring down your street and pulling up to your neighbor's house.

Everyone is looking out the windows to see what's going on.

You all see your neighbor being brought out in handcuffs.

Then you see another person on a stretcher. It doesn't look good.

The ambulance speeds off.

The police car with your neighbor in it speeds off.

One police car remains.

Now, how would you feel if that police officer went door to door and told you and the rest of the people on your street, who had nothing to do with the domestic dispute, that you had to disperse your parties, that everyone had to go home, and that there was going to be a curfew on your street from now on?

Would that be fair?

Of course not.

It seems ridiculous to even consider, when you look at all the facts involved.

Well, welcome to the situation in the Rock Island downtown right now.

Last Monday, the Rock Island city council voted 4-3 to indefinitely maintain a 2 a.m. closing time for nightclubs in the downtown. Nightclub owners were incensed. After having to suffer through the financial strain of covid, with their businesses already hit hard (many of them near closing, following the clubs that have already shut down including Billy Bob's and The Black Sheep), many of them felt the city was being unreasonable and unfair to the downtown clubs.

"This is ridiculous," said Terry Tilka, who owns RIBCO and 2nd Ave nightclubs, in a lengthy conversation we had after the decision. "They're killing us. They're killing the downtown."

The reasons for the continuation of the 2 a.m. given by both city council members and Rock Island Mayor Mike Thoms were that they felt it was best for the safety and image of the city and the downtown.

But is it?

Does the actual data match that rationale?

No. No, it does not.

And so, the next time the council meets, they should do the right thing, and put the closing time back to 3 a.m. They need to stop penalizing innocent business owners who have been doing the right thing.

Now, that said, I feel they should follow the same path as Moline Mayor Stephanie Acri, and use that 2 a.m. closing time as a penalty if a specific club is shown to be derelict in its duties to provide a safe environment. However, as long as a club is doing everything it can to

Stephanie Acri is mayor of Moline.

maintain a safe and secure environment, just like in Moline, it should be allowed to retain its 3 a.m. closing time.

Rock Island has been a mess already due to covid. Businesses have been open, closed, open with restrictions, closed again... it's been a terrible year. Nightclubs and entertainment venues have been especially hard hit, particularly spots like RIBCO.

"Covid took out our entire schedule, nobody's touring, we can't book anybody," Tilka said. "It's been like that for the last year. And now we've got to deal with this. How are we supposed to stay open when a lot of our business is in that last hour, that last few hours?"

Mayor Mike Thoms, in a lengthy conversation with me, addressed the various concerns raised by Tilka and other downtown club owners. Mayor Thoms also brought up a number of his own concerns, echoed by members of the council, about a potential rising number of problems in that midnight to 3 a.m. window, and how the number of incidents has been shown to rise in each subsequent hour. The study Thoms cited is certainly reliable, and its reach is nationwide, spanning data over a number of markets. I don't dispute the study or its findings.

But, other than in a broad overarching sense, is it relevant to this particular situation, and is this type of action merited?

As I pointed out to Mayor Thoms, saying that the chance of bar fights increases as people get more drunk is like saying your chances of getting wet increase the deeper you wade into a pool. This is nothing new. It's also nothing unique to Rock Island, or the Quad-Cities. Which is why, when bringing empirical evidence into the picture as a justification for action, you have to instead look at the micro-picture instead of the macro. You can't just generalize, you have to be specific in instances such as these, before making a sweeping judgement that needlessly penalizes those who don't deserve to be punished.

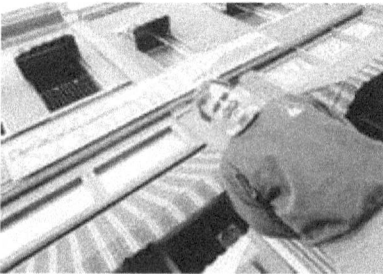

Terry Tilka is owner of RIBCO and 2nd Ave.

And when you look at the details of the data, and the context, a different picture emerges.

One which shows that the majority of the downtown nightclubs are safe, just as safe if not more so than any other nightclubs in the Quad-Cities, and, therefore, shouldn't be held to a more rigid standard.

If you've ever been to the downtown clubs, you can see this for yourself. As someone who has been to the downtown Rock Island clubs literally thousands of times, I can tell you, anecdotally, that the number of times I've seen fights and other violent behavior has been minimal, and certainly no more so than when I've been to Davenport, Moline, East Moline or Bettendorf clubs. I've seen thousands of shows at RIBCO and the next bar fight I see there will be my first. Same thing with Icons. Same thing with Big Swing, and its predecessor, The Blue Cat. Same thing with MD Green's, which is populated by an artsy crowd who are lovers rather than fighters, more interested in singing karaoke than anything else.

Have I seen some fights in the dance clubs? Yup, I have. Same as I have in dance clubs all across this country. And probably 98 percent of them involve drunk people in romantic entanglements. Which is to say, they're not random, they're tied in with a specific series of events, involving people getting too familiar with one another (or one another's significant others).

Those events have nothing to do with the nightclub owners. I should also note that those dance clubs tend to have a lot more security, and that those fights get broken up pretty quickly.

Is that a valid reason for closing the clubs at 2 instead of 3? People infrequently fighting over romantic entanglements in dance clubs?

I don't think it is.

But I'm only one person.

Will others agree with me?

Will others vote to help downtown Rock Island thrive again?

I guess we'll find out.

Dr. Seuss' Estate Did The Right Thing, And Created Another Lesson From The Late Author

March 5th, 2021

Think about the person you are now. You are a product of your time. Of your upbringing. Of your environment. Think about the person you were before the pandemic. Just a year ago. Different person?

Think about you 10 years ago. Different person?

How about 20 years ago or more, around the time of 9/11.

Different person?

We all evolve, we all change, according to our times, environments and circumstances. The question, as always, is how do we change and how much? Is it for good? Is it for ill?

This week, the estate of Dr. Seuss Enterprises, which controls the late author's books, decided to discontinue publication and licensing of six books by Theodor Seuss Geisel.

In a statement, they gave a succinct reason, saying, "These books portray people in ways that are hurtful and wrong."

A cursory glance at the books certainly backs that up. Each of them contain archaic stereotypical caricatures of minority cultures, including African-Americans and others, but overwhelmingly of Asian-Americans. All of them are wrong, and could certainly be hurtful, especially to kids, particularly to kids of those racial and ethnic groups.
Most of the books are not very well known. The only one which is pretty famous in Seuss' catalog is "And To Think I Saw It On Mulberry Street," which was Seuss' first book published, way back in 1937.

To say that social attitudes, especially those towards minority peoples, were different back in the 1930s is an extreme understatement.

Racism towards anyone who wasn't a white anglo-saxon protestant was pretty much de rigeur, and caricatures of all minority and ethnic populations, regardless of skin color, were abundant throughout the media, from books to daily newspaper editorial cartoons. If you went back into the archives of any local newspaper during that time, I guarantee you would find editorial cartoons with offensive caricatures and stereotypes.

That was 1937. Height of the depression, not all that long after slavery, right as the KKK was rising, just two decades after the first world war and the influx of immigrants into this country. Keep in mind there were people protesting and angry more than two decades AFTER this when young, handsome, rich, charismatic John F. Kennedy was running for president. Because he was an Irish Catholic. Imagine what it was like for people 23 years EARLIER who weren't white, handsome, rich, and charismatic. Not exactly enlightened and tolerant times. Racism was virulent and abundant in the 1930s and certainly the 1940s as we entered into World War II. And this is the era in which Seuss and his work was first born and evolved.

Because of that, quite frankly, it's more surprising to me that there weren't MORE examples of harmful and racist caricatures in Seuss' books.

Not because I think Seuss was a virulent racist, but because he was a product of his time, that time, in American history.

That's not to excuse it at all, but it is to offer some perspective.

And perhaps, another lesson, from the author's work.
I agree with the Seuss estate and publishers to remove those books with racist caricatures in them from his catalogue, although I would likewise agree with those books being re-released sans those images. Looking at the books, the overarching themes and images weren't racist, and removing the hurtful caricatures would improve them.

However, I also understand the decision to completely remove them as well.

This was a smart and compassionate decision by the estate of the author.

But it's also a decision that reflects the time in which his ancestors evolved, and our own society as it stands now as well, a positive lesson of how things can get better. And this is a lesson we can all learn from.

Dr. Seuss was a person of his time, as we all are, and I don't think he was willingly being hateful any more than I would condemn pregnant women pre-1970 who smoked or my parents and others like them who spanked their kids, or doctors in the early 1900s who prescribed morphine and cocaine to people. We're all the products of our times, and it's easy to see how those caricatures got into Seuss' work, since those racist archetypes were typical of most work of that time. The people weren't as enlightened or socially evolved. And, also, it's easy to understand how the vast majority of Seuss' racist caricatures were Asian, as Seuss was in the Army and worked with the military during WW II, when the Japanese were our enemies, and Americans were forcefully propagandized against Asian people.

I'm not saying he was right. I am saying that everyone is a product of their environment and upbringing and they reflect that, particularly in what they believe to be cultural norms. The question, as always, is what happens when those cultural norms change and evolve to be more enlightened. Do you continue to hold tight to archaic belief systems and biases, or do you open your mind and your life to new attitudes and pathways?

The Seuss folks obviously have decided upon the latter, and that's the right decision. I applaud them for it.

And obviously this is the lesson to be learned here.

We all make mistakes. We have all done things we cringe at in retrospect, or regret.

But all of our decisions and actions have one thing in common — they are the product of who we are and who we were at the time we made them.

Our lives, our perspectives, should be constantly growing and evolving as we encounter new information and outlooks. We should always be striving to be better people, to grow in a way that's going to create a better path for ourselves and a better example for our children and those around us.

But we're also limited by our background and our knowledge base and level of understanding at that time, and so we should look at those decisions we've made, and we should consider them and learn from them.
That's the lesson here.

That's the example the Seuss estate is setting, a new narrative, a new lesson, if you will, from the offspring of a man whose work was all about teaching those new lessons and getting people to think about the world around them and consider different perspectives.

Wherever he is now, Dr. Seuss is undoubtedly proud of his ancestors for that.

Because they've learned, they've evolved, and in doing so, they've made his legacy better and more in line with the overarching themes and subjects of his life's work.

As for those people who decry this as censorship, you are incorrect. They weren't censored, they made the decision to alter their own work, which is their right.

As for those who cry about how they shouldn't be changed, you are wrong. The caricatures were racist and harmful to children of those racial backgrounds, and if you're as big a fan of Dr. Seuss as you claim to be, you would know that an overarching theme of his work is inclusion, and he wouldn't want those kids to feel bad or alienated from the bigger messages in his work.

And as for those pundits who continue to push this ridiculous Culture War narrative to keep people angry and divided in order to desperately hold on to your fading audience or to distract people from what's happening in the corridors of power, you're all a bunch of ridiculous, histrionic buffoons and I hope your audience wises up and gains some perspective and context.

I would recommend they start by turning off the TV and reading and thinking about what I've just written.
And then maybe, actually reading some of Dr. Seuss' finer works, such as "The Sneetches And Other Stories," and considering them as well.

BREAKING: Quad-Cities Man In Park Enjoying Weather, Beer, Weed, According To Report

March 8th, 2021

BREAKING NEWS: A local TV news reporter whose name is being withheld for his own privacy and safety should government agencies and QAnon discover him breaking this clandestine and explosive information revealed on his Facebook today that while on assignment in the Quad-Cities, he encountered a man enjoying more than the pleasant weather today.

The reporter, who we will reveal is (to the best of our knowledge) not a part of the Deep State, revealed the incendiary information that he was, in fact, "sent out to talk to people about the nice weather."

(To those not "in the know," this is typical in journalistic circles, as once the weather becomes nice after a long and brutal winter, editors like to send reporters out to do what is known as a "human interest story" on topics of this nature.)

However, the reporter got more than he bargained for.

Much more.

Budweiser. The alleged "King of Beers."* (*DNA tests and family tree explorations pending.)

According to the reporter, who we will reveal is (to the best of our knowledge) not related to Brian Williams, Anderson Cooper, or Oprah, approached a man in the park.

He said, "I ask the guy "So what are you doing in the park today?" and he says "I'm just chillin', I smoked a joint and drank a big old Budweiser"."

The reporter also let is slip that this revelatory disclosure would NOT be included on the news tonight!

What are local TV stations hiding about local park patrons smoking joints and drinking big old Budweisers????

Does this have anything to do with Jeffrey Epstein, Tom Hanks, Q, or adrenochrome????

Keep your eyes on your eagle-eyed, steely-jawed, fearless muckraking local media source, QuadCities.com, for ongoing coverage of this IMPORTANT information you NEED to know!

The Pandemic Isn't Over, Remain Vigilant Over Covid And Let's Finally Get Through This

March 12th, 2021

There's an old saying that you shouldn't blame the messenger when you receive bad news.

However, that saying is reliant on the messenger being a neutral party.

When the messenger is merely the one bringing you the message, it's without blame.

For example, when we at QuadCities.com, give you a story featuring covid statistics, we're passing along information we've gleaned from an official source.

We also attribute that source, so that you know where we got that information.

We have no part in creating that information.

We do not make up the statistics.

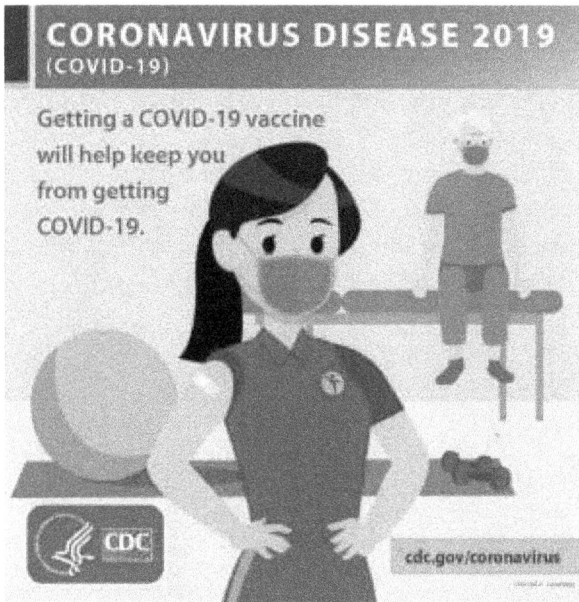

CORONAVIRUS DISEASE 2019
(COVID-19)

Getting a COVID-19 vaccine
will help keep you
from getting
COVID-19.

CDC

cdc.gov/coronavirus

The push is on to vaccinate as many people as possible against Covid.

We do the duty of what the media is SUPPOSED to do –
pass along information that's important so that it can be
seen by the widest audience possible.

What that audience does with the information is up to them.
The decisions they make are their responsibility.

It's our responsibility to be as accurate as possible within
our ability to present accurate information.

And that's what we do.

Like yesterday, when we ran a story about troubling
numbers on covid coming from the Rock Island County
Health Department. We did not make those numbers up.
We did not quote some flaky and dubious "professor" from
the internet or some alternate healer, we quoted actual

statistics from a reputable agency compiling relevant data, so that you could be informed on fact-based statistics and trends, to keep you and your loved ones informed and safe.

There are also times that we present opinion columns. These are clearly marked as columns, and should be understood as such. They contain factual information, and then take that factual information and formulate opinions based upon it.

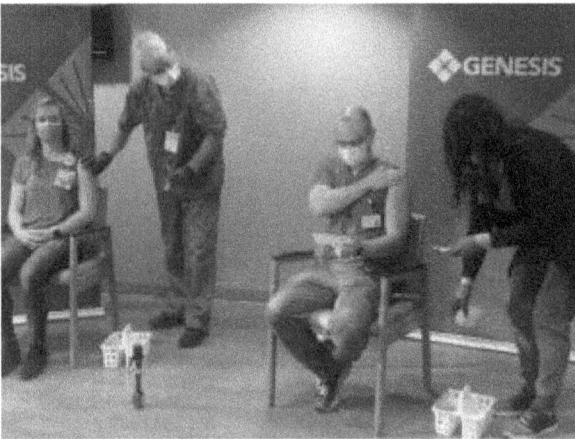

Genesis administered the first local vaccines in December.

For example, here's a column I wrote on Dec. 16, offering my opinion about what needed to be done to help Illinois and Iowa, and the U.S., more quickly get past covid-19.

In the column, I took the factual evidence before me, looked at and analyzed that evidence, and formulated an opinion based upon that evidence.

One of those opinions I wrote, on Dec. 16, was the following:

"It usually takes 2-3 weeks for infection numbers to spike after these types of gatherings. Well, 2-3 weeks after Thanksgiving takes us to mid-December. Then 2-3 weeks after the Christmas and New Year's Week takes us into mid-January."

I was taking a chance in presenting that opinion. But it was an opinion based in fact and analysis of factual evidence, which increased my chances of being correct. And, lo and behold, when you look at factual evidence and analyze it, your odds of being correct are increased, as they were in that column from Dec. 16, and as they had

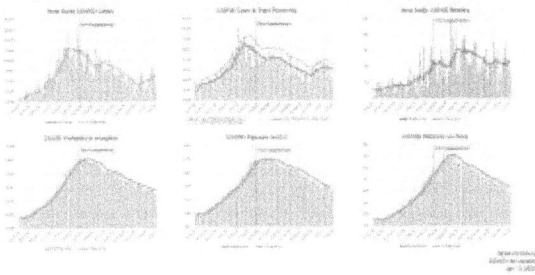

Tier 3 Mitigations Flattened the Curve in Illinois

The Illinois mitigations have helped flatten the curve for the spread of covid in the state.

been in previous columns I'd written.

In an earlier column in mid-November, I predicted cases would spike a week or two after Thanksgiving. They did. Iowa had a surge up to 19, 148 on Dec. 25, which is a surge of almost 2,500 cases over the day before, and reflects numbers spiking up.

Then I predicted cases would spike again a week or two after Christmas and New Year's Eve. And Jan. 8, two weeks after Christmas, we saw another surge, as Iowa hit 2,478 cases, which was its highest peak since – you guessed it – Dec. 18.

Now, the good news is, based on facts and data, I'm hoping that we don't get another surge. On the positive side, the mitigations put in place have worked, particularly on the Illinois side, which has seen its numbers dip mightily. That wasn't luck, that was science. That was Governor JB Pritzker following the data, telling people to take simple precautions, and enacting mitigations which worked to stop the spread and staunch the damage done. When Iowa Governor Kim Reynolds enacted mitigations last fall, it also worked. Funny, that, when you follow common sense precautions based upon science, it works out.

Covid-19 variant viruses have been found in both Illinois and Iowa.

And now we find ourselves on the edge of another era in regard to covid. Temperatures are going up, which is good news, as science has shown that higher temperatures slow the spread of covid due primarily to two factors — that the virus has a difficult time surviving outdoors in those higher temperatures, and because people aren't cooped up inside where they're more likely to spread the virus. In addition, vaccines are being administered on the regular, and the new covid bill about to be passed should fast track those vaccines even more, which should help move us towards herd immunity much more quickly.

However, we're not completely out of the woods yet. It's St. Patrick's Day this weekend, and a lot of people will once more be getting together. There are a number of variants to the virus out there that could complicate things. We don't know how much because viruses can be unpredictable, especially when they're mutating. Also, the original virus is still around, and is still a threat if people just completely go off the deep end and stop enacting any mitigations whatsoever.

We all want this pandemic to finally end. We all want things to go back to a more normal atmosphere. We all want to be able to go out, go to events, see our friends, have our businesses thrive again.

But that means that for a while longer, we still need to use common sense to get through this.

Wear your mask. Be smart in regard to social distancing. Keep your immune system up through vitamins, diet and exercise. And just exercise common sense. It's not that difficult.

Let's keep ourselves, our families, and the people around us safe — especially those people at high risk.

Let's get through this together.

Will Quad-Cities Covid-19 Cases Be Spiking In Two Weeks?

March 15th, 2021

I'm not great at predicting the stock market.

I can't say I've been especially adept at picking lottery numbers.

But I'm going to go out on a limb and say that Iowa Quad-Cities covid numbers, and probably statewide numbers as well, are going to see a rise in 10-14 days.

Over the weekend, my social media feed was flooded with pictures of people at the Mississippi Valley Fairgrounds, downtown Davenport, the Village of East Davenport, and really all over, enjoying the good weather and the premature St. Patrick's Day celebrations.

What did all of those pictures have in common?

Very few people wearing masks.

And almost none social distancing.

Pictures from the Mississippi Valley Fairgrounds St. Patrick's Day celebration. Trying to find masks is like attempting to locate Waldo.

Folks, we're still in the middle of a pandemic. Yes, I know that numbers are going in the right direction — Scott County has seen a decrease in positivity rate down to a consistent four percent over the past two weeks. Yes, I know the vaccine is rolling out and people are starting to get it, and President Biden has put the pedal to the metal in regard to making sure everyone has access to it.

But that doesn't mean there can't be setbacks, and the problem is, every time there is a setback, it's bad news for the industries and the people whose lives and jobs are negatively impacted by any shutdowns, limited or sweeping.

The entertainment industry in particular has been devastated by covid, and many people I know in creative and artistic fields are either completely out of work or very limited in what they can do. The one thing they, and the rest of the people in the industry, have in common is that we're all hurting financially from this, and have been for over a year now. We all want to work. We all need to work to pay our bills. We can't do that when so many things are shut down within our industry.

As always, some businesses and people have been responsible in regard to this.

But, of course, as always, some haven't.

Hey look, there's a handful of people wearing masks! And... a whole lot more without them!

And that's why, a year on, we in the U.S. are still stumbling through this while many other countries are not.

So when I see Facebook live feeds and pictures of hundreds of people standing around without masks, packed in drinking cheap beer to celebrate our national holiday of alcoholism, it's a little annoying.

I get it. It sucks. I used to love going out too. I still go out and do some things, but I try to be responsible about it. I wear a mask at the events, and keep socially distanced. I keep my immune system strong. I just utilize common sense. It's really not that difficult.

If there's anything we've learned over this past year, it's that people are going to do whatever the hell they want, regardless of data, science, logic and common sense. There's no vaccination program against ignorance and stupidity, so, don't expect that epidemic to end.

However, we can and should expect this covid pandemic to finally end at some point. The only question is when, and the answer depends on how we regard it over the next few months. President Biden has set a goal date of July 4 for some semblance of a return to normalcy. Will we hit it? Will we see independence from the pandemic, finally, or is this going to continue to drag on needlessly?

I don't know. Like I said, I'm not psychic.

But I am cynical. And so I know how I'm betting.

This Being Canceled Is The One Thing That United America

March 17th, 2021

We continue to live in a divided country.

People on the far right and far left continue to battle each other over incredibly important and vital issues that are key to our nation's survival.

Subjects like the gender of plastic Potato Heads and whether or not Tom Hanks is a giant lizard who sucks the blood of children keep the battle lines fiery and blazing with anger and animosity between the two sides.

But there's one thing we can all agree on.

One cancellation that made us all happy, regardless of our politics, religion, or whether or not we like pineapple on pizza.

And that is the cancellation of Caillou.

If you are a parent, you shudder at the mere utterance of the word.

If you aren't a parent, you still, subconsciously, feel a chill and an unexplained desire to go to the store to stock up on condoms.

I don't think I'm exaggerating to say that Caillou is everything that is terrible and demonic in the world, and everything that needed to be stopped.

The animated child star of his eponymous PBS series, Caillou is a mean, annoying, bald little shit who has been driving parents to drink since his show's debut 24 years ago.

Pure evil.

Caillou is terrible, and you will not convince me otherwise. Every whiny, excruciating, annoying thing about him labels him as the purest spawn of Satan we've seen on the television since perhaps Scrappy Doo. Fortunately for me, as a parent, I was largely spared his darkness. My son watched Caillou once, and thankfully did not like it. In fact, he would turn off the TV when it came on.

It was one of my proudest moments as a parent when he first did that.

Still brings a tear to my eye.

No, my son did not subject me to the horror of Caillou. I just had to see the little brat in commercials and promos while my son was watching shows he actually liked on PBS.

But not all parents were as fortunate as I.

Many parents have confided in me their despair over having to watch and endure Caillou in all his whininess and terrible splendor.

However, not all is lost in regard to parents' ongoing battle against Caillou.

In fact, the battle may in fact be already won.

Earlier this year, Caillou was actually cancelled.

Yes.

Finally, a cancellation we can all agree upon.

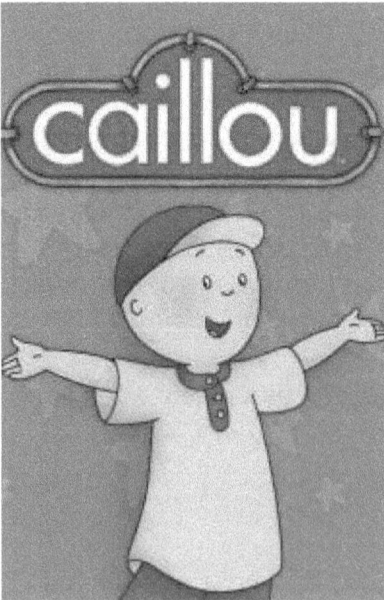

Whether you voted for Joe Biden or Donald Trump, we can all agree that Caillou was terrible. Oh, and also that Jeffrey Epstein didn't kill himself.

In January, the announcement was made, and, now, in March, the last episodes of Caillou have finally bid their farewell on PBS stations across North America.

In some ways, we can thank some elements of cancel culture for this.

Since 2015, parents have been complaining and protesting the cueball-headed little beast's show on PBS, due to the fact that he sucks. Specifically, they mention that he's mean, exhibits sociopathic behavior towards his family, and does things like smacking his babysitter and lying to his parents. The repeated letters and calls were enough to get four episodes of Caillou's show banned.

It was a start.

Over the ensuing five years, momentum began to build, with more and more "Stop Caillou!" and "Cancel Caillou!" petitions being sent to PBS.

Until, finally, something magical happened.

The little brat's show was finally pulled from the air.

Even this dude was crying tears of joy when "Caillou" got cancelled.

There was no fond farewell show. Caillou wasn't seen moving away, or growing up, or being swallowed up by a black hole, or attacked by wolverines.

It was just gone.

Thus sparing current and future parents a nightmare which had been going on since the '90s.

And so, if it somehow seems, over the past couple of months, that things have been a little less testy, a little less venomous, in the divides between people in this country, perhaps that's why.

Perhaps we just all needed a cancellation we could agree upon.

Because nothing unites people like a shared hatred.

And nothing ever united most of America like its hatred of Caillou.

Happy Birthday To A True Quad-Cities Creative Entrepreneur: Anthony Natarelli

March 19th, 2021

There's a sarcastic meme going around on TikTok in which a guy brags about making a million dollars in the "stonk" market.

After a show of bluster and ego, he begins going into details on how he did it. He starts by showing off his portfolio of one million, and then says, "I started when my Dad loaned me two million, and a month later, after all my investments, I've got a million dollars!"

It's funny, but it's also true. And it's often overlooked when we're considering people that the media tells us to regard as massive successes in the business and entertainment world. So many of them started with inherited money and a head start on things, and they just spun their brand off of that.

Whether it's the Kardashians or Donald Trump, it's always easier to be a success when you begin with several million dollars in the bank. You don't have to worry about failure, and you've got the capital to begin in a place far ahead of most which have to work arduously for years to amass that type of head start.

That mainstream media emphasis on those born of those circumstances, and the media's laziness in pointing out the inherent advantage of them, draws an occluded line in drawing a picture of real success. It also diminishes the real efforts and the much more arduous task of those who actually live up to the mythology of the self-made entrepreneur, who are very often ignored by that same front-running mainstream media.

Anthony Natarelli, left, plays Carl and Mike Turczynski played Jody in "Lonely Planet."

One of those people who actually lives up to the standard of being an entrepreneur and one of distinctly spartan work ethic and manic creativity is Anthony Natarelli.

Natarelli celebrated a birthday this week, with very little fanfare outside of his circle of friends and the random messages on his Facebook page. But as the local actor/comedian/musician/producer/etc. marked another year around the sun, it was interesting to look back upon his previous 365 days, and unfortunate to think of how little credit he's been given for all he's accomplished during that time, and those previous years before.

I first met Natarelli back in 2015, when I directed him in a series of sketch comedies. He was a regular performer for my production company, My Verona, as well as Tristan Tapscott's various productions for District Theater. But beyond that, he was a jack of all trades and an interesting creative talent who should've, at some point, gotten a lot more recognition than he's been accorded.

Natarelli acted in "Something Intangible" at Playcrafters, with Bruce Duling, in July 2019.

Natarelli has been a fantastic actor over the past few years, giving incredible performances in shows from "Rocky Horror" to "Hedwig," but it's his strange and singular entrepreneurial tangents which have set him apart from most and which have been, sadly, his most ignored ventures.

Natarelli was one of the first creators, along with Khalil Hacker, to quickly identify the emerging trend towards virtual theater, particularly during a pandemic which wiped out live performance as we knew it, and shuttered up every theater in the Quad-Cities and beyond. Natarelli's $1 Producer Project began putting out more video and multimedia productions, culminating in the brilliant comedy/drama "Lonely Planet," this past summer, which was staged and filmed in Natarelli's apartment.

The project showcased all the talents for which Natarelli should be far more lauded and recognized than he is — it's brilliantly acted and directed, cleverly staged, and demonstrates a vision and creativity of incredible energy, the kind of imaginative electricity which helps

Anthony Natarelli in his apartment set for "Lonely Planet."

invigorate an arts scene, and which is sorely needed, especially after the year we've had in which the arts have been hobbled by covid.

Natarelli followed that up with a pair of complete and utter oddities which were nevertheless hilarious and welcome in their absurdity and unique nature.

"Khalil's Covid Christmas Special" and "The Unofficial Tabasco New Year's Spectacular" were both amazingly strange, random and funny, the type of dada-ist absurdism that seemed perfectly appropriate to end the woebegone chimera of a year of 2020. Neither of them gathered a titanic audience, but those that watched them definitely enjoyed their bizarre humor and off-kilter world.

But, again, as with most of what Natarelli pulled off in the past year, they were audacious and admirable, albeit largely ignored.

It's unfortunate, because it's people like Natarelli, and various others like him in the local scene in recent years — Khalil Hacker, Andrew King, Jon Burns, and more — who have produced some of the most innovative and interesting creative projects. And yet they're typically overlooked, often in lieu of those who are able to make a bigger splash.

Khalil Hacker in a scene from "Khalil's Covid Christmas Special."

In part because they're more generously financed and more uniformly praised and recognized within the mainstream.

However, eventually, hopefully, that's going to change.

It was about twenty years ago, that I met and began working on short comedy films with a couple of young local filmmakers, Scott Beck and Bryan Woods, who took about 15 years to become "overnight

Anthony Natarelli

successes" with a little movie called "A Quiet Place." Since then, they've struck big with another film, "Haunt," and just wrapped up their first big directorial effort, "65," which stars an actor you might have heard of — Adam Driver. At one point Scott and Bryan were pretty much unknown as well, and yet they kept on plugging away, making films, doing what they loved, creating interesting and cool projects, until eventually they got their break.

Some folks never get that chance. Some folks never get that break.

I'm hoping Natarelli does. He's one of several creative types on the local scene I think have a talent that should be given far greater recognition than it currently holds. But, like so many of them, he's a struggling artist, who's got to pay the bills, and is running on that never-ending treadmill to keep up while pursuing his dream.

A dream that's a lot harder to pursue when you're the head of the one dollar producer project, rather than the one million dollar producer project.

But there are some things, like talent, like vision, like imagination, that are incredibly valuable in their own right, and he, and many others on our local scene, are rich in those.

Keep that in mind, as the doors begin to open for local businesses in the coming months. Keep those folks in mind, the people doing the offbeat and quirky and imaginative things. We write about them all the time here on our own shoestring budget entrepreneurial project, QuadCities.com, alongside some of the higher profile attractions around the area. Mix it up, give them a try, check out something they're doing, something strange and new and exciting. You never know, you might find something you never knew you loved.

Oh, and Happy Birthday, Tony. I'm looking forward to seeing what your odd and warped imagination has in store for us this year. Cheers!

Grammy-Winning Artist's Disgusting Song Should Definitely Be Cancelled

March 21st, 2021

This week, I took some time off from my job and household obligations to sequester myself in an ashram to fully focus my rage on a Grammy-winning song of such wanton lust, indulgence and disgusting perversity that I couldn't even.

That's right. I couldn't even.

And they haven't even created a drug for that yet. But I hear there are a number of Hollywood celebrities that are going to be doing a zoom cover of, no, not "Imagine," but "You've Got The Touch," to raise awareness and sympathy for those who can't even.

Anyway, I digress with that important information.

Once I got over not being able to even, I managed to harness my rage over this disgraceful and morally depraved song, and started posting online that the artist behind this Grammy debacle should be cancelled. Pronto.

I'm happy to note that Candace Owens, Tucker Carlson, Tipper Gore, and Joel Osteen all retweeted my opinions, and agree with me 100 percent. This song and its artist are pushing this smut to kids and they must be stopped. And we, and others like us with nothing better to do, are the ones to stop them.

Of course, I'm talking about the Grammy-winning song "Eat It," by Weird Al Yankovic.

Now, you might be saying, "But Sean, that parody of Michael Jackson's 'Beat It' came out in 1984, and won the Grammy the same year, after becoming the biggest hit for Weird Al up to that point, and spawning an award-winning video which launched him to mega-stardom and positioned him as the top-selling music parody artist of all time!"

The American single version for "Eat It." Note demonic red, and Illuminati black, white and red colors.

And I would reply, "Thank you for that expository sentence that lets people know who the hell I'm talking about if they're completely out of the loop, or are members of Gen Z who don't know who the hell Weird Al Yankovic is."

I would also reply that cancellation and moralistic posturing knows no expiration date. If someone once did something that offended someone at some point, no matter when it was, it's open game.

Then, after that reply, I would get back to my outrage.

That outrage is centered around the fact that Weird Al's "Eat It" is nothing more than a lewd, lascivious fandango glorifying that most debauched of all the seven deadly sins, gluttony. It celebrates unhealthy overeating and influences young people into a world of obesity and potential pre-diabetes, and its video is nothing more than what you might see in a strip club with an all-you-can-eat buffet. Which is an extremely insensitive thing, because there are hard-working strippers there who are trying to make money, and not only does that buffet take away from their potential earnings, it makes them smell like steamed eggs and ham,

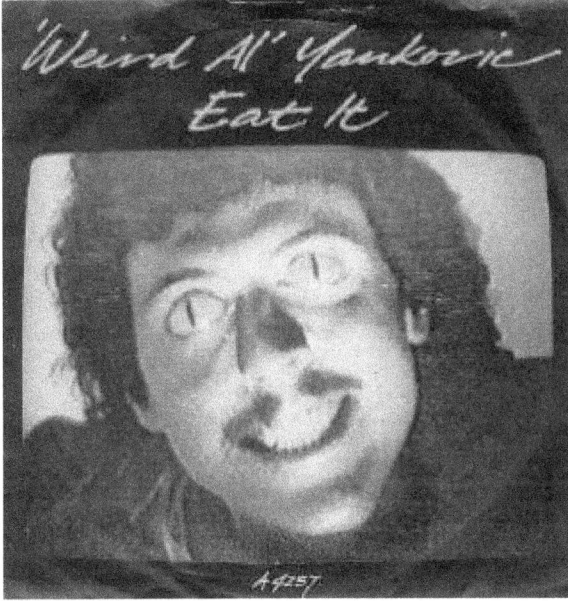

The British cover version of Weird Al's Eat It. What, the American version wasn't good enough for you damn tea drinkers? Christ. USA! USA! USA!

and they do not like that, Sam I am.

Weird Al's wanton tune talks about <u>wet ass vegetables, stopping and dropping into a seat for an all-you-can-eat spaghetti dinner, and chants and glorifies the fact that there are s'mores in this house, there's some s'mores in this house</u>.

Seriously, this is the kind of thing that can not only corrupt an entire generation, or several, since it happened in 1984, but bring down an entire country. And really, folks, has the U.S. been the same since 1984? Think about it. The wealth gap has grown completely out of control. The cost of living has spiraled upward while wages have stagnated. The U.S. has endured several presidencies which have been marked by lies, scandal, and controversy. We've pretty much been in a never-ending series of wars since then. There was 9/11, and economic crashes after every Republican presidency, and a freakin' pandemic for cryin' out loud! And when's the last time Christopher Cross had a hit? Not after 1984 he didn't! Jesus Christ, whatever happened to that guy???

I blame all that on Weird Al and his satanic, and Grammy-winning, "Eat It."

So I ask you all, to please join me, and Candace, and Tucker, and the rest of the Fox News crew, in uniting against this incredibly important national scandal which threatens to rock the United States to its core. We'll be doing a bus tour around this country to raise awareness for the cause, and rally proud Americans against this outrageous attack on our staunch morality and pure way of life.

Our bus will be coming to your town soon. It'll be easy to find.

It's the bus that'll be blasting "WAP" on a continuous loop from the radio.

I Sure As Hell Hope Rock Island County Board Knows What It's Doing With The Courthouse

March 25th, 2021

And so the saga sort-of, maybe, kinda, possibly, ends.

Or not.

We'll see.

The Rock Island County courthouse saga has gone on for a couple of years now, with the county wanting to demolish the building and repurpose the spot just off the bridge,

Protesters outside the courthouse calling for it to be saved.

and a growing number of citizens calling for it to be sold to local developer Joe Lemon, who has been trying to buy it for over a year.

We at QuadCities.com have covered this issue extensively, and if you want to get more of the details, I encourage you to listen to my various QCUncut podcasts of a meeting about the issue, an interview with board member Kai Swanson which discusses it at great length, my interview with Lemon about it, and my first and second interviews with community activist Bridget Ehrmann, who deserves a lot of credit for tirelessly working to bring this issue to the forefront and into the public arena for debate.

Whether you agree with Ehrmann or not, you have to admire the fact that she's not getting paid, she has no financial interest in the matter, and yet she's been working diligently on this issue. That demonstrates a passion for the community and a strength and courage of local altruism which is definitely admirable.

Agree with her or not, she deserves respect for her efforts.

As I've said with my interviews with all parties, and as tends to be the case with me, I see this far more as an issue of self-interest than I do of altruism.

As is usually the case, I am not Princess Leia trying to save Alderaan,

I am Han Solo, looking out for what's best for himself and fighting alongside the rebels as it suits my own interests.

Local developer Joe Lemon has been attempting to buy the courthouse for over a year.

I suspect many of the board members who voted for the sale of the courthouse to Lemon are likewise "flying Solo," especially given many of them are pro-business and privatization Republicans, standing politically at odds with Ehrmann and her group, which tend to run more Bernie-style progressive, yet are facing off against a largely establishment Democratic block against the courthouse sale. It's a strange mix of alliances and antagonisms. But that's politics, which lead to unorthodox alliances, and that's how deals are made in the real world, between adults, who overlook the programmed superficial tribalism for their own interests and goals.

I have nothing personally for or against the courthouse. If I had to judge it upon my experiences within it, I don't have a lot of misty memories. I think the courthouse is great and all, it's a fantastic building, an example of stunning architecture and a testament to the brilliant craftsmanship of times gone by. But the building that means more to me is my own home, and what means more to me is the rising amount of county taxes I pay on that building I own.

As I've said to Ehrmann, I greatly admire her cause and energy in pursuing it, but the main thing that tips the scales for me towards her side is that from a financial standpoint, I felt the sale of the building to Lemon, the putting of money INTO the county coffers rather than taking it out for demolition and new development, was a better deal. I've said the same to Swanson, although he's countered that he and his group feel that in the big picture, financially, the county demolishing it and repurposing the land, will be the wiser financial move.

Bridget Ehrmann

Whoever was going to win, I was hoping was going to be right. Because when it comes down to it, I, and most people in the county, are sick and tired of rising taxes, and we want our tax bills to be reduced.

At this point, it looks like the ostensible winners are going to be Swanson and those on the board who support not selling it to Lemon.

Again, I disagree, I would've voted to sell it to Lemon. But, that's what happened with the vote. Whether or not that changes, we'll see.

But either way, here's the thing, especially when you're a public official: You're rarely going to make everyone happy, and you're often going to make people angry, but WHEN YOU MAKE A BIG DECISION, YOU'D BETTER HOPE TO HELL YOU GET IT RIGHT.

That's how I feel about the Rock Island County board with this courthouse thing.

I thought they should've sold it to Joe Lemon, gotten some money out of it, let a reliable developer with local ties renovate it out of his pocket and using state and federal grants which weren't going to reflect upon OUR property taxes. But, obviously, the majority of the board disagreed with me, and many other people in the county.

Ok, that happens. BUT… whatever you do with that space, you'd better damn well make sure it pays off. And given its location, right across the bridge, as the visual and aesthetic gateway to the city, you'd better damn well make sure you get the optics right as well.

Green space? Park? Something cool and aesthetically pleasing, as Swanson told me they were looking to do when we spoke on my podcast? YES. I'm fine with that. It doesn't bring it tax revenue, BUT it also improves the city from an aesthetic standpoint, which could, ostensibly,

Kai Swanson

lead to a more positive environment in the downtown which could also lead to more business development, which does bring in tax revenue.

But if they build a juvenile detention center, as has been rumored? HELL NO.

The last thing the city needs is a kid jail welcoming visitors right off the bridge. Given that Rock Island is already struggling to overcome an undeserved negative reputation, we don't need the sight of incarcerated children in the shadow of the WELCOME TO ROCK ISLAND sign.

The City of Rock Island has been doomed by bad decisions over the past 20 years (Walmart, anyone?), but now, the county board now has an opportunity to make a good one. I may not agree with them now, I may not agree with their decision not to sell to Lemon, BUT if they do something great to help the city and the county with this space and it's both fiscally responsible and aesthetically pleasing, I'll certainly admit I was wrong.

We'll see what happens.

I hope I have to apologize, rather than saying "I told you so."

Because the first is only going to cost me my pride.

The latter will be a much bigger hit to my taxes, and my checkbook — and to yours as well

Advice To A New Teenager

March 26th, 2021

It seems like only yesterday when I turned 13. I remember it distinctly, from my party with my friends to some of the gifts I most cherished (a Converse All-Stars Magic Johnson t-shirt, a Duran Duran album, and other things which would certainly date me as a child of the '80s.)

This week, my own son, Jackson, turns 13.

And it's a much, much, different world from when I entered my teen years.

I didn't have cell phones, or the internet, or anywhere near the entertainment or virtual reality options my son does now. I spent most of my time playing outside, my mom was working most of the time and my siblings and I basically raised ourselves like a pack of clueless wolves.

My son has had a much different, and in many ways better, life than I, and I am grateful for that. It's always been my goal for him to have a better life than I had, and to be a better person that I am, or have ever been. Low bar, that, on the second, but, still.

He is undeniably the best person I've ever had the honor of meeting, and I'm looking forward to continuing to experience the adventure of his life with him. And as that time goes by, he may ask me for the advice I've gained in my years before him and since he's been born.

142

That's why I started writing this list of things I've learned and I wish my parents had told me. I started it shortly after he was born, and I've added to it and published it every year on his birthday since, and, now, I've published it in a book, called, shockingly enough, Advice To My Son, which is available on Amazon.

As I look at the list, it's good advice for me to follow as well. And, in thinking about the times we're living in right now, it's just good advice in general.

Here are some of the important things I've tried to impart upon him:

A friend is someone who is with you when you have nothing to offer them but your friendship.

Remember the people who are with you when you're down. They're the only ones who deserve to be with you when you're up.

It's never a bad thing to be a good, respectful person. In the end, you're the one who has to look at yourself in the mirror, and if you can say you did the right thing, you'll always be able to do that and smile.

Always keep an open mind, until you need to close it.

People will show you who they are, if you let them, and you have the patience to observe. The question is, do you want to see people as they really are, or do you want to see them as you want them to be, using the shorthand of what they reveal with your imagination and desires for what you wish them to be filling the gaps?

You aren't what you say you are, you are what you do.

Anyone can destroy, but it takes a greater person to create.

If anyone ever asks you what you want to be when you grow up, tell them you want to be happy. If you're happy, everything else just kind of falls into place.

Someday, someone is going to break your heart. It will tear you apart. It will make you feel awful. But somehow, somehow, try to retain the thought that this, too, is a positive thing. You're not meant to be with them if they don't want to be with you. And by leaving you, they're giving you an important gift – the freedom to potentially find the person with whom you ARE meant to be.

What do you look for in a significant other? Someone who makes you happy as much as possible, because life's too short and your time is too important to be with someone who makes you unhappy more often than not. Someone who makes you proud of yourself and your actions when you're with them. Someone who you're proud to be with. Someone who brings out your best, but stands by you at your worst. Always remember, you don't have to be with anyone to be happy or complete. You can be happy all by yourself. So choose carefully, and pick someone who is going to add to your life, who is going to make it a better place far more often than not.

When you're going out on a date, remember these things: Be nice, be polite, be yourself.

Someday, you may find yourself in a difficult part of life, going through some hardship. You may look back at previous times in your life when things were much better. The pessimist is going to think "Look at how much better things were. I'll never be that happy again." The optimist is going to think "Look at how much better things were. If I was that happy before, I can be that happy again." Always be the optimist. Life changes, circumstances change, but as long as your faith in yourself remains the same, and as long as you move forward and make positive decisions, you can always get your life back on track.

While going through those difficult times, always remember that there are things you can control, and things you can't control. Worry about the things you can control, and always try to do your best in making them better. One thing you can always control is your thoughts. Try to make them happy ones – think of things that make you laugh, jokes, friends, happy memories with people you love, like your Dad. Those will make you smile and laugh and once you're smiling and laughing, no matter what, your life is going to be at least a little bit better.

Always keep a treasure chest of happy memories, jokes, funny movie scenes or funny things in your head that you can always turn to when you need a laugh. Whenever things aren't going great, pull stuff out of that treasure chest, think of those funny jokes and good times. And whenever you experience something that makes you laugh or makes you smile a lot, file it away in that treasure chest. It'll be the best investment you ever made.

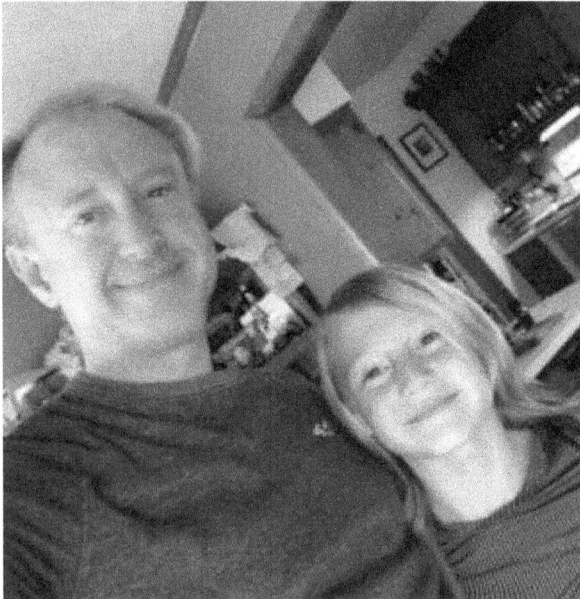

If someone treats you badly, more often than not, it's because of them instead of you. If you treat people politely and with respect, and they treat you badly, you have nothing to feel bad about. Don't waste your time with those people. Don't bother planting flowers in concrete, and if you do by mistake, don't waste your time trying to water them.

It takes a while to eschew the security of labels, until you realize labels hold no security. Everything from wedding vows on down has been broken and discarded, worthless. The only way to know if something is sure and true is if you both realize your life would be profoundly diminished due to the absence of the other, and that there's no one with whom you could imagine spending your time and having as much joy and love in your life.

The strongest bonds are forged when traveling on narrow paths.

Sometimes things aren't too good to be true, they're just good and true.

Really, when it comes down to it, you either see your life as a miracle or an accident. You won't find out whether you're correct until you die, but your answer will go a long way in determining your happiness while you're alive.

Criticism is just someone else's opinion. Just like yours.

If you can make yourself laugh, you'll never be completely unhappy.

The best gift you can give yourself is your own love and friendship. You are a wonderful person and you have every right to be happy with yourself. If you can be, then you'll never truly be alone. You'll always have yourself to keep you company.

Always remember at least one really funny movie quote. One line that never fails to make you laugh or smile when you remember it. You'll need it when you're at your most down, to remind you that life brings laughter as well.

Along the same line, always have at least one really wonderful memory to hold on to, to cherish, and to remind you of the beautiful things in life, and that no matter how sad you might be at any given time, life has the potential to bring great happiness too. I hope I've given you enough of those good memories to last a lifetime.

The best way to say you're sorry is to consider your actions before you commit to them and decide not to do hurtful things in the first place, so you won't have to apologize later.

Good things can happen to anyone. But first you have to believe they can happen to you.

It's always better to be hated for what you are than loved for what you are not.

Life isn't about finding yourself, it's about creating yourself.

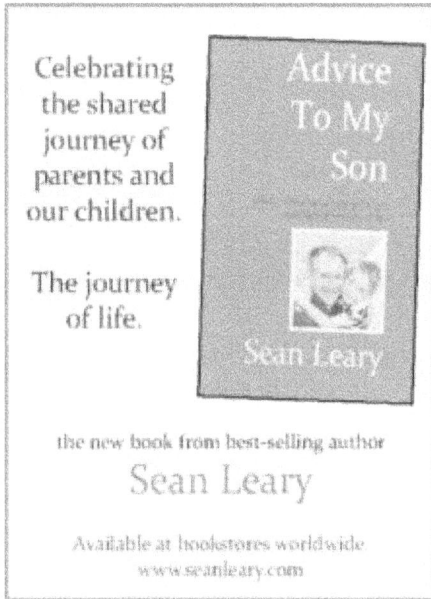

Celebrating the shared journey of parents and our children.

The journey of life.

Advice To My Son

Sean Leary

the new book from best-selling author
Sean Leary

Available at bookstores worldwide
www.seanleary.com

There are some people in life that are always optimistic, no matter what, and some people that are always pessimistic, no matter what. Always make sure that you surround yourself with as many of the former as possible. It'll make all the difference.

Always make sure you have plenty of creative people in your life. You'll never want for surprises.

Don't be afraid to believe the good things people say about you. It may always seem easier for the bad things to stick, but both are opinions, so why not allow the good ones greater weight?

Friends are people who make your life better for being in it. If they don't, and what's more, if they consistently make your life the worse for being a part of it, they're not worth having in your life. There are eight billion people in this world. You can find better friends. You don't need anyone who brings you down and isn't worthy of you — or even more important, who isn't worthy of the person you want to be.

The same goes for the person with whom you're in a relationship. They should make you a better person for them being in your life, and you should do the same.

Every day when you look in the mirror take time to notice your positive attributes. Concentrate on them. Celebrate them. Allow them to take greater prominence than those negative things you may feel the self-defeating need to dwell upon. Life is too short for you to make yourself unhappy.

It's not "mean" or "selfish" to retain some self-worth and expect appreciation and reciprocation.

You are a valuable person.

You are an important person.

You are worthwhile.

Don't forget that or allow anyone to convince you otherwise.

Never underestimate the power of discipline and perseverance. The difference between those who accomplish things and those who talk for years about wanting to accomplish them, but who never do, is that the former know how to translate words into action and maintain their direction in doing so, regardless of the inevitable obstacles that come their way. And remember that even taking small steps every day eventually finds you much farther along than not taking any steps.

Consider the ramifications of your decisions. Every decision, big and small, sets you on a path. It sends you towards one thing and away from another. Often, the larger the decision, the bigger the sacrifice of other options. So if you're going to choose one thing over another, be damn sure that the thing you're choosing is worth it, and will be in the long run.

Whenever you get advice, consider the source. People's worldviews and attitudes tend to impinge upon their opinions. If someone is in an optimistic state, they'll tend to give more good and upbeat advice, and will tend to be more supportive of positive actions you might be taking. If they're in a pessimistic state, they'll tend to be more negative and cynical about both positive and negative actions. Take all advice, but keep that in mind and add as many grains of salt as needed accordingly if someone with a pessimistic slant always seems to be shooting you down without good reason.

The journey of 1,000 miles doesn't begin with a single step. It begins with the thought and the conviction that you are going to take that step.

No matter what you do or where you go I'll always be thinking of you. No matter how old you get, I'll always remember you as the tiny blessing you were the day you were born. And no matter what, I'll always love you.

And that's love: When you're always there for someone, and you always want to be.

Lil Nas X Is Just Triggering People For Attention. And, Predictably, They're Giving It To Him

March 29th, 2021

So, the latest ridiculous pop cultural controversy out there is over the Lil Nas X "Montero" video, which has right wing conservative social media throwing holy water, exorcisms, and epithets in equal measure at the singer who shot to fame with "Old Town Road."

As one person cried on Twitter, Lil Nas X has completely disappointed them because their kids loved "Old Town Road," which also featured Billy Ray Cyrus, whose daughter, Miley, has been the target of some of these same holy rollers trying to condemn pop cultural provocateurs.

Which is… EXACTLY WHAT THEY WANT YOU TO DO.

This whole thing is an obvious and blatant publicity stunt.

And, honestly, I love it for that.

You want to get some attention? Tweak a group with a short fuse and a big mouth. Either extreme — right or left wing — will do. Trigger them with something, and just watch as your Google search ranking goes up, as clueless morons throw fits over your button-pushing and give you all the attention you desire for your new project.

And that's all this is.

The "Montero" video is a massively produced, expensive bit of CGI publicity stunt meant to hype a so-so song with meh lyrics that hit upon a topic as well-tread as that old town road.

It's blatantly obvious the song is your typical tune written by an artist that's just achieved massive fame and realizes that it's not all it's cracked up to be, and feels like they made a deal with the devil, and they have to work hard to retain their sense of self and creative control in order to overcome the demons of the entertainment industry.

Only, Lil Nas X paints that picture LITERALLY in the video.

In the vid, which probably cost millions, the singer plays the part of Adam in the garden of Eden (i.e. an innocent musical artist), seduced by the devil (i.e. the music industry), and corrupted along the way (i.e. poisoned by the industry), before retaliating at the end and, after lap-dancing Satan (i.e. pretending to go along with the program of the industry), taking the crown of hell and ruling as leader (i.e. taking over creative control of his work and becoming even more famous than before.)

This song, video, and subject, is beyond beating a dead horse, it's a horse corpse frappe. Probably 90 percent of ALL artists, after their big breakthrough, write some song or album about how the industry is grinding them down and how fame isn't what it's cracked up to be, whether it's Stone Temple Pilots' "Big Bang Baby" (which is a really cool song and video), or the awesome Sex Pistols' "EMI," or Pink Floyd's "Have A Cigar," or Nirvana's "Rape Me," etc. etc. etc.

And in this case, for whatever reason, Lil Nas X has decided to name his industry protest album after something that sounds like a car endorsed by Ricardo Montalban in the 1980s. Which makes it even more difficult to take seriously.

As for the video, and its scandalous imagery?

The Lil Nas X "Montero" video is FREAKIN' HILARIOUS. It's so over the top ridiculous and contrived to offend, it's impossible to take seriously. It's totally batshit crazy and intentional, and it always amuses me to see provocateurs push the buttons of the easily triggered, which is all he's doing here.

I mean, c'mon, he makes out with a gay Satan in the Garden of Eden, then slides down a stripper pole to give the devil a lapdance, before killing him and taking his crown of weaves.

How on earth could any reasonable human being take this seriously? Honestly. It's so blatantly a button-pressing joke and publicity stunt.

And yet, there are millions of people out there, taking the bait, saying that Lil Nas X is somehow indoctrinating gullible teens into demonic possession and gender fluid activities with entities from hell.

But, that's also the point of the antagonists, that this is entirely a symbiotic relationship.

Fox News and all the rest NEED people like Lil Nas X. For the same reason Lil Nas X and artists like him NEED Fox News and the other right wing pearl-clutchers. One peddles outrage to an audience that gets off on being outraged, the other blatantly peddles the thing to outrage to curry favor with an audience that wants to be shocking and get a rise to make their mark in the world. It's like a shark and a lamprey, only with more glitter and outtakes from the "Spawn" movie.

And good on him. You go Glenn Coco, four for you, Lil Nas X. You fire up that outrage, you create that controversy, you work those album sales.

But no matter what you do, no matter how far you go, you'll never quite generate as much controversy as this guy and THIS VIDEO...

Happy Birthday To Two Legendary Quad-Cities Entertainment Spots: CoOp And Rozz Tox

April 1st, 2021

Two icons of the Quad-Cities indie scene celebrate birthdays today, as Moline's CoOp Records and Rock Island's Rozz Tox are both blowing out the candles (Rozz Tox' are probably on cupcakes), and although they're both suffused with a spirit of fun, their success is serious testament to hard work and an example of how to do local business right.

It was 26 years ago that music scene fixture and die-hard Replacements fan Reid Robinson decided to take the leap and open up CoOp at 3727 Avenue of the Cities, Moline. Little did he know he was getting in when the getting was about to get anything but good.

The mid-'90s were the last heyday for music stores. There were several already at the mall, a handful of indies and on top of that you had big boxes like Best Buy, Walmart and Target getting into the biz, much to the chagrin of those shops that specialized in music and related entertainment. But the 900-pound gorilla of online music, perhaps first

157

writ large by Napster, but only to state the obvious trend, was right around the corner.

Within a decade, the vast majority of music stores in the Quad-Cities and elsewhere would be dead.

And yet CoOp survived.

Survived and thrived.

Things haven't gotten better in terms of music shops. Malls are now mausoleums and their once-smiling Sam Goodys and Musiclands are resting in pieces, their inventory shipped off to warehouses and other retailers. Most shops that reigned in the time of Hootie and the Blowfish have aged about as well as, well, Hootie and the Blowfish.

But CoOp has remained, in large part because it was always more than a music shop. It was a vibe, an experience, a destination location. It had the mainstream stuff, sure, but it had what the real music fans wanted, that rare object of affection that you couldn't get anywhere else. It had character and personality. It hosted live performances and local record release parties and sold various and sundry accompanying paraphernalia. It was, and is, unique. You go into CoOp and it's "High Fidelity." It's what you see in a movie where the script calls for a music shop of distinct persona and an intimate understanding of the fetishism of music fandom.

There's no place like it in the Quad-Cities.

And that's the point.

The same could be said for today's other birthday biz, Rozz Tox, which began TEN years ago (doesn't seem that long!) with Benjamin Fawks opening up a little coffee shop/café/performance space/hangout in a long dead-end section of a town that was headed in the wrong direction.

By 2010, downtown Rock Island had past its last peak as the It spot of the Q-Cs. The '90s and early-mid '00s were the heyday for The District, but once the shiny new things of downtown Davenport and the Village began to sparkle, people began giving the cold shoulder to downtown Rock Island, and once Moline started to show some signs of life in its downtown, Rock Island really began to wane, quickly.

And that was right when Fawks decided to open Rozz Tox at 2108 3rd Ave., Rock Island.

Good recipe for failure, right? Business opened in a declining part of town, a downtown on the way down, and in a spot way off the strip.

And yet . . . it thrived, and still does.

Why?

Same reason for CoOp – Rozz Tox provides something that's unique, that's distinct to the Quad-Cities and certainly Rock Island.

It's got a personality, it's got a character, it's unlike anything else.

160

Like CoOp, I've very much enjoyed my times at Rozz Tox. My son, Jackson, has had his artworks displayed there in a kids' art show. I've been interviewed there by Andrew King for his live, on-stage talk show, and I've returned the favor by interviewing Andrew for my own gigs. I've read fiction and poetry there at open mic nights. I've gone to raves there. I've seen movies there. I've watched awesome live music there. And I've had some great food and drinks there and just hung out, getting work done and visiting with friends.

If you look at that list, you'll notice it features a pretty eclectic group of activities. That says a lot about Rozz Tox. It's open and varied and eclectic enough to include an incredibly diverse array of entertainment, but it retains a certain vibe, a certain character, a certain personality.

It's interesting to look at these two businesses, and it highlights something very important about the business landscape nowadays.

You look at both of them, and both of them should've, by conventional wisdom, failed.

One began just before the complete cratering of its industry, killed along with most retail shopping, by the onslaught of the internet and its ubiquity in our lives.

The other began as a spot in a town and area on the downward slope, branded as a cool hot spot when all the people who would ostensibly be interested in something of that ilk were seemingly spending all their time in other, far more hyped locations being trumpeted as the places to be.

161

But both defied prognosis and common wisdom because common wisdom is only good at predicting the common, and these locations are anything but.

And that's the lesson for success in this era, when everyone is torn in so many different directions by a seemingly endless cavalcade of options – when people can go anywhere, you need to give them someplace to go unlike anywhere else, and when they can get anything, you need to give them something they can't get anywhere else.

And that thing, that irreplaceable thing, is a feeling, a vibe, an experience.

You go into CoOp, you get a distinct vibe, a unique experience.

You go into Rozz Tox, you get a distinct vibe, a unique experience.

That's been the secret to their success.

When you make yourself just like everyone else, there's no reason for anyone to choose you rather than anyone else.

But when you stick to your own path, when you stay weird and stay unique, then you offer a destination that can't be found anywhere else.

So happy birthday to CoOp and Rozz Tox — two of the places that make the Quad-Cities unique, because they've had the courage to always be themselves.

Will Acri's Mistake Open The Door For Rayapati In Moline's Mayoral Race?

April 1st, 2021

Stephanie Acri apparently has a very short memory.

It was just four years ago, that previous Moline mayor Scott Raes was set to pretty much cruise to re-election. He'd done a pretty good job as mayor, voters seemed to like him, and there didn't seem to be much reason to switch leadership for the city.

Bob "Mr. Thanksgiving" Vogelbaugh being interviewed by WVIK.

Then Raes made the monumentally huge mistake of contesting the candidacy of one of the most popular men in the Quad-Cities, "Mr. Thanksgiving," Bob Vogelbaugh (as well as Acri's candidacy) over a ridiculous technicality that they didn't number the pages in their applications. Once it got into the media, and people found out the whole story, they were furious that Raes was giving such a hard time to a guy, Vogelbaugh, who'd dedicated a large portion of his life to helping people in need get a hot meal on Thanksgiving. Vogelbaugh dropped out, but people were still so pissed at Raes, that Acri ended up winning on a write-in vote.

A write-in vote! You know people really have to be ticked at you for you to lose on a write-in.

And they were. And the irony of the whole situation was that if Raes had just stayed on a positive path, in touting his accomplishments and successes as mayor, and not given any attention to his opponents, Vogelbaugh and Acri, he very likely would've won.

The same could be said for Stephanie Acri.

The current mayor has had a pretty good run of it. She's had some good, she's had some not as good, but overall, public sentiment in Moline seemed to be leaning towards re-electing her over challenger Sangeetha Rayapati.

Then Acri, to coin a phrase, "pulled a Raes."

A dark money organization began pushing out a flyer to Moline residents slandering Rayapati over a decision she was part of as president of the school board. That decision was regarding a Moline teacher who mistakenly posted a video of themselves having sex on Snapchat.

According to reports, the teacher most definitely did not mean to post the video, and it was on Snapchat unintentionally for 15 minutes until multiple of the teachers' friends who saw it contacted them and they, frantically, immediately took it down.

Stephanie Acri

Was Rayapati one of the people having sex in the video? No. Was Rayapati the teacher? No. Did Rayapati post the video? No.

From the sounds of it, the sex video was not specifically made for nor recorded on Snapchat. The teacher had a private video on their phone. Is that a crime? No.

The teacher somehow, probably through ignorance of technology or something of that ilk, ended up very mistakenly posting that video to their Snapchat. Is that a crime? No. It's just dumb, and shows an ignorance of the forum.

Some of the teacher's students saw the video, took screenshots of it, and according to reports, even discussed whether to notify the teacher it had been posted to warn them it was there. Is that a crime? No, again, stupid mistake on the teacher's part, and maybe not the best judgement to add current students to your Snapchat, but given today's remote learning environment, somewhat understandable.

As reported, a friend of the teacher on their Snapchat saw the video, and frantically called them to tell them, at which point, after it had been up 15 minutes according to reports (there's an Andy Warhol joke in there if you care to find it), the teacher quickly removed it. Is this a crime? No, and in fact, it corroborates that the teacher posted the video unintentionally.

The police, recognizing that this was more of a stupid mistake of someone naive to the technology and not an intentional act to groom underaged students or distribute pornography to them, wisely decided not to press charges.

The school board, of which Rayapati is president, also recognized the same thing, realized it was a dumb mistake, and put the teacher on leave. Personally, I'd recommend reassigning the teacher to another school where the students haven't seen them boning on the 'chat, but, maybe that's down the line. Was this a good decision to put them on leave but otherwise not push it further? Yeah, I think it was.

And this story was reported and all out there in the open, as much as it could be, legally. The police are public employees. The school board are public officials. All of them are paid for by the taxpayers. And therefore their meetings and documents are public record, subject to freedom of information requests and open to the public.

Now, one of the things Rayapati is being attacked on by Acri and the dark money flyer, is that she "covered it up" by "not commenting on it."

Morons, please.

Sangeetha Rayapati

Now, either Acri and the dark money folks are completely ignorant of the law in regard to human resources (which is very disturbing considering Acri is the mayor of a large city), or they are engaging in disingenuous and ridiculous pearl clutching to rile up people too stupid or ignorant to know the law in regard to employees' rights.

Because, as anyone, like me, who has run a business, and who has been called for a reference knows, YOU CANNOT LEGALLY COMMENT ON EMPLOYEES' TERMINATIONS OR PERSONNEL ISSUES. You can't. You can confirm they worked there, you can confirm their start and ending dates, and you can answer whether or not they are eligible to be re-hired. That's it. You can't go into details. You can't comment on whether they were disciplined for mistakenly posting a sex video on Snapchat.

If you do, you could be sued. And so in NOT commenting on the issue, Rayapati is not only doing the right thing, she's also saving the school board and the city money by saving them from a potentially major lawsuit which would be paid for by the taxpayers.

Rayapati is doing the wise and smart thing.

And yet, she's being criticized for it.

The flyer sent out made it sound as if Rayapati was the Lil Nas X of the Quad-Cities, intentionally corrupting the minds of innocent students by setting up an amateur teacher porn ring on Snapchat and just letting it go wild as she stood back and cackled, presumably as she wished for a handlebar mustache she could twirl.

Now, dark money organizations are notorious for doing this around the country, because we live in a country where most politicians are whores for the rich and they've set the system up to allow for unlimited money to have influence over people stupid enough to base their decisions on asinine flyers that show up in their snail mail box. I've seen a ton of them in the months leading up to elections, full of lies, capital letters, and bad photoshop, and I give them all the consideration they deserve in the few seconds before they get thrown in my recycling bin. Most reasonable people follow the same path. But unfortunately, apparently, there are still gullible people out there who believe this crap.

But Acri should know better. Acri should remember how she got into office in the first place — through a stupid mistake by her predecessor, who was headed to re-election, the same way Acri probably was prior to this.

Acri, asked about the flyers, should've said the following: "The issue with the teacher has been dealt with by the police department and the school board, and since it's a personnel matter, I can't officially comment on it in detail. As for the flyers, I had nothing to do with them being sent out, they were sent out by a private group."

That's it. If a reporter asks a follow-up question, you refer the reporter to contact the people who sent out the flyers.

There ya go. Advice from a public relations professional. Something that probably would've been helpful in this case.

Instead, Acri made the mistake of doubling down on the misleading and incorrect messages of the flyers and making an even bigger deal out of it. She told WHBF-TV4, among other comments, "My opponent has falsely accused my campaign of sending mail to residents that is critical of her record and her lack of leadership."

That's all you need to say to get people curious. To get them looking into this. To give your opponent more attention that they otherwise wouldn't have gotten if you'd downplayed it.

And the thing is, once people actually learn all the details, they see that Rayapati's record and leadership are actually shown in a POSITIVE light in regard to this incident. Rayapati showed GOOD judgement, echoing the good judgment of the Moline Police Department and States Attorney who, it should be very highly noted, DID NOT PRESS CHARGES AGAINST THE TEACHER. If law enforcement found nothing wrong, then why would Rayapati and the school board? If charges were filed, if the teacher was convicted, that's a different story. But no charges have even been filed. From all indications, this was a major screw up by the teacher, but not one which was intentional and therefore a fire-able offense.

So in actuality, Rayapati's record should not be criticized in regard to this, and in fact, she showed good leadership. She investigated the incident, involved the police and States Attorney, there was a thorough investigation done, and she did it without exposing the school board and the city to expensive litigation by violating the human resources personnel contract or the teachers union contract of the teacher. Her actions to ostensibly "cover it up" were precisely the RIGHT thing to do in this instance.

Will people recognize this, and will it turn the tide for Rayapati in the mayoral race? We'll see.

Will Acri continue to push this issue, thus giving Rayapati even more attention that she wouldn't have gotten otherwise, and allowing more people, like me, to actually look into this and see that Rayapati did the right thing? We'll see.

But regardless of what happens, this was a political mistake for Acri. She should've learned from the mistake of Raes. If you're in the lead, you don't look back. You keep going, you keep pressing forward with your own positive record and agenda.

Oh, and one more thing — you make sure your Snapchat doesn't have access to your phone's photo and video files.

Mike Thoms And Thurgood Brooks Showcase The Best Rock Island Has To Offer

April 4th, 2021

I got two election fliers in the mail the other day. Being that we're only a few days away from the April 6 election, and the mayoral race in Rock Island is, from most reports, closely contested between incumbent Mike Thoms and challenger Thurgood Brooks, this is not surprising.

Thurgood Brooks

But what has been pleasantly surprising is the positive nature of this campaign.

While the Moline mayoral race slides around in the mud, with a bunch of slanderous and poorly spelled fliers by a dark money group peddling lies about Stephanie Acri's challenger, Sangeetha Rayapati, the two men vying for Rock Island's mayoral spot have maintained a refreshingly positive and progressive campaign, both of them highlighting their strengths, and in some instances pointing out their differences, but doing so in a civil manner that's impressive and heartening.

You look at fliers and publicity materials for both Thoms and Brooks, and they're filled with endorsements and substance, talk about what they'll do if elected, proactive and positive material on their own strengths, rather than slanderous falsehoods about their opponent.

It's nice to see.

Knowing both men, I'm not surprised. I've spent significant time interviewing and talking off-the-record with both Thoms and Brooks, and I've found both of them to be great candidates and people who I personally like very much.

I will not be divulging my vote (which has been determined after much, much inner debate), nor will I be endorsing a candidate, because I think both of them, if elected, would do a phenomenal job.

Mike Thoms

Brooks brings a vibrancy, energy, and a welcome rush of ideas and enthusiasm to the race. He's run a terrific campaign, and has demonstrated a wonderful vision for Rock Island and its future. Someday, he's going to be a great mayor of this city. Will that be Tuesday? We'll find out. But regardless of the results of this election, his youth and exuberance is very welcome on the local political scene, and I look forward to seeing where he goes. I think if he's elected, he's going to be a force to be reckoned with, an energetic and positive leader to take the city in a very progressive direction. It'll be a learning curve for him, and will take him a little while to get everything down, given his youth and lack of experience, but given his family's background in local politics and Thurgood's own indomitable personality, I think he would do a great job.

Mike Thoms has likewise done a very admirable job in a thankless and precarious position. When he was elected, the city was an absolute mess, the result of poor leadership prior to his tenure. On top of the financial boondoggles he's had to wade through, he got hit with the economic knockout punch of covid and its devastating impact upon Rock Island. And yet, Thoms has remained the perfect man for this time in our city's history. If there's any one word you can use to describe Mike Thoms, it's steady. He's extremely level-headed, logic-driven, and solid. During these times of turmoil, he's had the perfect demeanor to deal with the chaos. He's been very transparent with the electorate — he's appeared numerous times on my podcast, QCUncut, to answer any and all questions posed to him by citizens, and has been very open with the media and through us the citizens of Rock Island. (As has Brooks, it should be duly noted.) And regardless of the challenges faced, Rock Island, under Thoms' leadership, has made progress, which is quite impressive given the obstacles he's faced.

If Thoms is elected to another term, I expect much the same in regard to his stable stewardship. He's had to make tough decisions many times, but has been open to explain them and take responsibility for them, which is what a public servant should do. I would imagine if he's elected again, he'll keep doing so, while continuing to lead Rock Island in a positive direction. The one major disagreement I had with Thoms was over the privatization of the city's water and sewer system, which I feel should be completely off the table — an issue with which Brooks agrees strongly with me, one of many agreements I have with Brooks. However, in looking at Thoms' record and personality, it's certainly

Jack Cullen of the Quad Cities Chamber will be the new downtown Rock Island director starting April 1.

fitting of his level-headed character to listen to offers and different information. Thoms insists that's as far as it's gone, and if he wins another term, I would hope he's going to keep his word in regard to that, as I feel the sale of the water and sewer would be a massive disaster for Rock Island. Otherwise, I like a lot of what Mike's done, especially in his partnership with the Quad Cities Chamber, and their hiring of the very capable and impressive Jack Cullen to lead the downtown renovation. I very much look forward to seeing what Cullen and downtown area alderman Dylan Parker can do together. They're both talented, smart, and pragmatic. We at QuadCities.com definitely look forward to working with them to help showcase and spotlight the wonderful aspects of Rock Island, particularly in the downtown.

Regardless of what happens Tuesday, the main thing to remember is that we're very fortunate as Rock Islanders to have a terrific selection between two very strong candidates. My hope is that regardless of who wins, the two of them find a way to work together to help build back the city they obviously both love.

And once more, my kudos to both men for running such a clean, positive, and admirable campaign against each other. The contest has been proof that two candidates of different political perspectives and backgrounds can engage in a contest about ideas and vision, comparing and contrasting with one another without lowering themselves, and in doing so, raise up the city both of them represent so well.

I wish both Mike Thoms and Thurgood Brooks the best of luck in this Tuesday's election, and I strongly encourage all Rock Islanders to go out and vote for their preferred candidate. This is a case where our city cannot lose regardless of who wins, and honestly, as someone who has lived in Rock Island for 25 years now, that's a wonderful feeling to have.

Who Should Be The NBA MVP? The Answer Might Surprise You... (Hint: NOT LeBron!)

April 8th, 2021

We're entering the home stretch of the NBA season and along with talk of playoffs and playoff seeding (more on that in days to come), here comes the speculation on post-season awards firing up.

The biggest award, of course, is the MVP trophy, which causes the greatest debates and in many ways generational rifts among sports fans.

There's a highly vocal contingent of mostly younger sports commentators who absolutely worship LeBron James, and their media companies make millions off of clickbait articles unreasonably and unfairly comparing him to Michael Jordan.

There is no comparison.

This is nothing against LeBron, who I think is a terrific player, and is a great off-the-court person and personality, it's just that you really can't compare the two players. They've played in different eras, they've had very different careers (Jordan playing for the same team and growing with that team and building it up into a contender; James jumping from super team to super team to play with other established stars), and their styles are very different. LeBron is much more of a Magic Johnson style player. He's a facilitator with a big body who can also score. The more apt comparison to Jordan is Kobe — they're both aggressively alpha scorers with similar personalities and styles.

But I digress.

But I digress to prove a point, that the media has been preoccupied with lauding LeBron for so long that they've become blind to the fact that his game has slipped. He's gotten older, there's no shame in that, it happens to every player. But if you watch as many NBA games as I do, and that means watching a LOT of Lakers games, because they're on constantly, then if you're looking at things objectively you have to see that LeBron has gotten slower, he's taken more plays off, he's not the same player he used to be. Sure, he's still good and he still flashes signs of that talent, but he's not the overwhelmingly dominant player he once was and therefore should not be in consideration for the MVP trophy as some commentators have deludedly and mistakenly put him. He shouldn't even be in the top ten.

So, who should be, and why?

Glad you finally got around to asking! Quit talking about LeBron for clickbait!

In order:

10. Zach LaVine: The Bulls are still on the playoff bubble, but they've made major strides from the car wrecks of the last few seasons, and it's largely due to the emergence of LaVine as a superstar. He does everything for the team,

taking leadership, taking all the big shots, bringing the ball up and facilitating most of the time, and, up until the trade deadline when Chicago made a handful of fantastic moves to get more veteran leadership, LaVine was the unquestioned veteran leader of one of the youngest teams in the NBA. The Bulls should make it into the playoffs this year for the first time since Obama was president, and it's going to be largely because LaVine has kept them in the conversation to get them to this point.

9. Stephen Curry: Curry has been remarkable on the court, as usual, now that he's back and healthy, to lead a disjointed and young Warriors team that's in the midst of an on-the-fly rebuild. Much like LaVine, Curry is unquestionably the man for Golden State, and has not only taken on that responsibility, he's also kept the younger and rougher players upbeat with his ebullient personality and joy for the game.

8. Luka Doncic: Honestly, you want to talk about LeBron carrying teams? Who is the Kevin Love or Kyrie Irving for Luka Doncic? Who is the D-Wade or Chris Bosh? Hell, who's the Dennis Schroeder or Montrezl Harrell? Dallas, aside from Doncic, is a terrible team of underachievers, not-much-achievers, and the oft-injured and inconsistent. Doncic is a remarkable talent, and deserves better. Here's hoping Mark Cuban finally surrounds him with some decent players so he can finally get the credit he deserves. The fact that Dallas is a solid playoff seed with that craptastic roster tells you everything you need to know about how good Doncic is.

7. Giannis Antetokounmpo: Giannis likewise carries a team which would barely be on the playoff radar without him. He's been stellar this year, although he started off slow, which put him behind in the MVP race a bit. Also, it's

tough to justify putting him in the top six over the guys I've got in there. He'll probably get his third MVP at some point, and hopefully he gets a championship, which will be a mammoth achievement given the Bucks' decent but hardly awe-inspiring roster, but not this year.

6. Donovan Mitchell: How is this guy never mentioned in the MVP conversation by national commentators? I know he plays in Utah, and y'all don't give a crap about the Jazz, but Jesus, what does he have to do? The Jazz have had the best record in the NBA, by far, all year, and Mitchell is the best player on the team, a terrific facilitator and alpha scorer. I'd have him higher, but the Jazz has more of a team game, and so it's not as obvious in regard to Mitchell being the guy carrying the team. But still, give the guy some love already.

5. Devin Booker: Same here! Everything I said about Mitchell also applies to Booker. Yeah, there's no questioning Chris Paul has been huge for the Suns, who only have the second-best record in the NBA, and have for most of the year. But if you watch the Suns, it's obvious Booker is the man. Paul provides veteran presence and leadership, but Booker is typically the guy in the spotlight racking up the biggest shots, and he's the ascendant star on the team. I'd put Paul around 11 or 12 if this list went out that far, but like LeBron, he's showing his age, especially on defense (also like LeBron), and Booker is the one you've got to recognize for the Suns massive resurgence, which goes back to the bubble last year before Paul ever showed up.

4. James Harden: I find it very ironic that the same NBA commentators who drool all over LeBron, who hasn't won big without assembling a team of stud players around him, crap all over James Harden for forcing a trade out of

Houston, which was going nowhere. Harden has been phenomenal for the Nets, leading them and building team chemistry while Kyrie and Durant were injured. Harden's most underrated aspect of his game is his ability as a facilitator, which should be apparent given that he's leading the NBA in assists, but is often overshadowed by his transcendent scoring abilities. The Beard deserves some major recognition in the MVP rankings, and if it wasn't for the fact that Durant and Kyrie are back and taking some of his shine, Harden would be higher on this list for me.

3. Joel Embiid: This is the guy I had at number one most of the season until he got hurt, and for good reason. Because I've watched a lot of 76ers games! All you had to do is watch more that a couple to see that Embiid was the MVP. Incredibly dominant player leading a very good team which wouldn't be nearly as good without him. Embiid is a fantastic talent, and still might get the trophy, but the long time down injured is going to dock him points. I'd still be happy seeing him get it though.

2. Nikola Jokic: He's right there at the top, and I think he certainly deserves the MVP in my book, but my number one has done more to carry his team to its ranking. Jokic is a remarkable talent — a phenomenal passer for a big man, great shooting touch, just a terrific player. He looks gangly and awkward at times, but the guy just gets it done, and in many ways he's a throwback to classic post centers who were good passers and would distribute from the post. But he can also hit the three, get boards, and play good defense. Right now I'd say Jokic is, deservedly, the guy who the national voters will give this award to this year, and I've got no problem with that. He's 1B with me in terms of my ranking, but I can't deny the pick I've held all season.

1. Damian Lillard: Every big shot. Every last second game-tying or game-winning shot. How many times has Lillard taken them for the TrailBlazers? EVERY TIME. And how many times has he hit them? Pretty much EVERY TIME. Lillard has always been one of my favorite players, an amazing scorer and creator who's been criminally underrated because he plays for Portland, but this year he's been out of his mind. With the Blazers few supporting stars injured for most of the year, and Lillard operating with a roster that, on paper, looks like it should be fast-tracked to the lottery, Lillard has carried the Blazers throughout the year, keeping them in the top eight in the west throughout. When have the Blazers NOT been in the playoff picture in the west? Never. Despite all the injuries, they've always been in the mix. Dame Time is why. The guy has done pretty much everything for the team, and gotten little to no recognition for it. Finally, FINALLY, he's starting to show up in some MVP conversation, but he should've been there all along. No doubt, Embiid and Joker are very, very deserving of the trophy. But to me, there's absolutely no player in the NBA which has carried his team to such lofty heights with as little help as Lillard. Damian Lillard should be the NBA MVP for 2021.

And there you have it.

Agree with me? Disagree? Leave your own picks, praise, complaints, and arguments in the comments.

Now, let's enjoy the rest of the season and into the playoffs!

The Real Secret To Great Pictures: Buttcheeks

April 9th, 2021

It's that time of year again, and if you have kids in elementary school, you know exactly what I mean.

School pictures time.

That's right, that time when you get your kids all dressed up and tidied up and get their hair looking perfect and their outfits looking spot on and send them to school, and then six or eight weeks later you get a packet of pictures that features a child that looks fantastic, but has a look on his or her face somewhere between fear, disinterest and a desperate need to pee.

I've been pretty lucky over the years in that my 13-year-old's pictures have been pretty good. But he's had his moments. Including last year. It's not a bad picture, it just looks like he's thinking, "hurry up and take the damn picture already!"

And it's really sad.

Not just because these pictures are being memorialized in yearbooks that will end up in the bottom of boxes in the attic and landfill (hmmm, ok, put that way, maybe it's not such a tragedy), but it's because the pictures could and should be so much better if the photographers would master a very simple way to improve school pictures instantly.

185

School photogs, I have one word for you.

That word?

Wait for it.

Wait for it.

I think I said wait for it, didn't i? Well, you're not waiting for it. When I said wait for it, I mean wait for it. I mean WAIT. WAIT. FOR. IT.

Ok, you've been patient enough.

That word?

Buttcheeks.

Yes, buttcheeks.

Ladies and gentlemen, I see this every spring — the continued scourge of children not smiling in school pictures. The half-smiles. The surprised looks. The attempts at a grin. The frowns.

This could all be cured with one thing: The proper use of the word buttcheeks at just the right time, said or exclaimed a second or two before the picture is being taken, to make a child laugh or smile at the absurdity of the moment and the word.

Now, there are specific ways to SAY buttcheeks that will get even bigger smiles from kids, dare I say guffaws, sincere grins and hearty chuckles. A funny intonation, mock indignation, an accent, etc. These will all accentuate the call of the wild buttcheeks and make for consistent

186

laughter and compelling, joyful school pictures year after year.

Why, you might even throw in the phrase poopy butts from time to time to mix things up. Once you've reached expert level.

But take it from me, the expert use of buttcheeks is not only a sacred responsibility, it's an honor, a calling, really, and should be taken lightly. Especially if we're going to stop this annual scourge of less-than-stellar school pics.

So, school photographers, don't let us down.

Buttcheeks. Learn it. Live it. Love it.

Use it liberally as needed to make the school yearbook pictures of American children once more the envy of children around the world! Make our school yearbooks great again! Make them great with buttcheeks!

Trust me on this one.

No, really, trust me.

Do I have to go through this again.

Ok, good.

God bless you. God bless America. And of course, God bless BUTTCHEEKS!

Smoking The Controversy On facebook That Everyone Is Talking About

April 13th, 2021

There's a controversy on Facebook that everyone is talking about.

I know, shocking! What is it, a Tuesday?

Yes, actually it is.

Quick, pick up your dry cleaning before they close. You're welcome.

Of course, every day there's a new controversy on social media. The social media companies pay people to engage and stoke controversies and then they push them through their algorithm to people they know will get ticked off, to get people fighting, and that's how they draw bigger audiences, and make more money.

The previous paragraph was brought to you by…

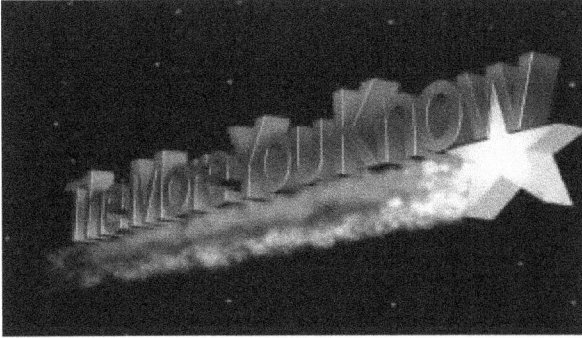

But today's controversy is particularly gouda, and has drawn some sharp contrasts you chedda know about.

It was started by well-known local troublemaker and former Dispatch/Argus Food Editor Brandy Welvaert.

Usually, Welvaert, typically drunk on the cooking sherry stash she found in a secret underground bunker below previous food editor Liz Meegan's desk, would spice her Facebook by peppering out japes and jibes about soups, pork t sandwiches, and a mysterious fellow named Jeff.

However, this week, she's done something even more eyebrow-waggling.

TRIGGER ALERT!

WARNING: DO NOT GO ANY FURTHER IF YOU ARE NOT PREPARED FOR SOMETHING WHICH COULD POTENTIALLY SHOCK AND STUN YOU.

OK, YOU'VE BEEN WARNED.

Are you sitting down?

You should be.

TRIGGER WARNING: Brandy Welvaert and her smoked lactose intolerant post.

Because I'm telling you: This week, Brandy Welvaert slammed foods labeled as non-smoked.

Yeah.

I'll give you a minute.

Ready? Ok. Deep breath now. Find your center, get those chakras in alignment, clutch the crystals tighter, surround yourself with that happy place, and we'll continue.

The dairy diva posted the following on her illicit Tome of Countenance:

"I do not personally feel it is necessary to label foods as non-smoked if they are non-smoked. I believe only foods that are smoked should be labeled as such.

#fightme

#yourown #personal #cheeses"

Maybe it's because she asked for it, but people started fighting her. And she cut the opposition into blocks, or, sometimes individually wrapped slices.

Is that a cow, or SATAN????

A cheese fan identifying himself as "Nathan Williams," retorted to the boiling Brandy, "I believe most provolone is smoked, maybe that's why they labeled it? On a side note, pre-sliced or shredded cheese is heresy."

The wild Welvaert was not o-queso with that. She slammed back with bleu language, shredding this alleged "Nathan Williams," with, "This is a good point; however, I stand by my opinion that non-smoked foods need no label. I am immovable on this, as you can plainly see. Now, onto the heresy; I support heresy of all types. Refute if you must."

From there, the conversation went savage, as people began bringing up smoking parmesan, and mozzerella, and I think someone even mentioned a brie and a bit of Old Croc smoked cheddar.

Before long, the whole comments section was like that scene at the end of "Event Horizon," only with people fighting over cheese, or, maybe it was more like this Frankie Goes To Hollywood video.

But it was all because of that cheeky rabble-rouser Brandy Welvaert.

Liz Meegan is not smiling at you now, Brandy.

I tried, oh, I tried to stop her. But she was raging too hard.

"Such a risky topic to cover!" I mentioned.

She melted my mild suggestion, retorting, "Exactly. It is. But I have never been one to shy away from strong opinions, no matter how unpopular. Don't get me started on shake canister parm!"

You've been warned, folks.

You have been warned.

Tomorrow on Facebook: We get Brandy Welvaert started on shake canister parm. Fasten your aprons.

This column is dedicated to Liz Meegan, one of my favorite people, and former employees at the <u>Rock Island</u> Argus.

Unlike Brandy Welvaert.

UFOs Are Real. The Government Has Confirmed It. Are We Just Going To Ignore This?

April 17th, 2021

There's a phrase, whistling in the dark, describing someone scared who is taking any number of glib, superficial actions to avoid confronting the fact that deep down, they're frightened out of their minds.

This phrase is reminiscent of much of the media right now, as this week, and several times over the previous few months, the United States government and the U.S. military has admitted the existence of UFOs.

This is not a joke.

I'm not kidding.

There isn't a punchline at the end of this column, as there usually is.

The U.S. government, the Pentagon, has admitted the existence of UFOs.

Now, don't get me wrong, I'm not saying they've admitted the existence of alien beings. Only the craft, which by literal definition are Unidentified Flying Objects.

But that, combined with the evidence presented, should be enough to be worldwide news, occupying the 24-7 cable channels for a long stretch, and far bigger news in this country than it is.

An image of a UFO in radar released by the Pentagon.

While the national media is happy to go nuts with wall-to-wall coverage of Lil Nas X's Satan shoes and video, or a handful of old Dr. Seuss books being put out of print, the UFO story has barely registered a blip, and then it's been quickly shunted aside for more substantial coverage of weighty subjects like Kim Kardashian's ass.

This phenomenon really started in earnest last year, when the Pentagon admitted they had evidence of a number of UFO sightings and have, for over a decade, had a top secret organization looking into the unidentified vehicles. U.S. Sen. Marco Rubio — you know, the legitimate political veteran who just ran for president a few years ago, not some freak in a tin foil hat like Lauren Boebert — requested a detailed analysis of the task force's findings. A year ago, the New York Times ran an article on the phenomenon and the program, quoting an astrophysicist and former consultant for the UFO program, Eric W. Davis, as saying that he gave a classified briefing to the Defense Department agency regarding "off-world vehicles not made on this earth."

Again, this is the Pentagon.

New York Times.

Marco Rubio.

Various images of UFOs have been released by the government and authenticated as real.

These aren't fringe elements or websites that look like they were made on AOL in 1997 featuring obviously photoshopped pics of Bigfoot waving as his flying saucer leaves the Taco Bell drive-thru.

These are legit media sources, legit organizations, saying that UFOs exist, and at best they really have no freaking clue what they are.

However, they have admitted to discovering and testing wreckage from them.

Whaaaaat???

Again, WHY ISN'T THIS BIGGER NEWS??? I'm really kind of stunned that more people haven't picked up on this and it isn't all over the cable channels. After all, now that Trump isn't president anymore, tweeting red meat out to both sides of the political aisle, what do they have to really talk about?

Oh yeah, that's right, Satan shoes.

This is most astonishing when you consider that news keeps slowly leaking out, and the most recent included actual video of a number of triangular objects above an aircraft carrier, taken by the Navy. That joins a number of other videos which have been not just released, but identified, as noted here on a video compiled by CNN, which got surprisingly little traction on that 24-hour-a-day news network. That joins various other videos which have been leaked and talked about in the media.

This video was released by the Navy, showing a number of triangular objects that remain unexplained.

Now, I get it. This isn't just big news, it's got the potential to be incredibly world-changing, and that's frightening to a lot of people. Even if the UFOs aren't aliens from another planet or another dimension, the entire concept is scary, because the alternate explanation is that another government, most likely Russia or China, who are antagonists to the United States, has this kind of advanced technology, which is a daunting prospect. Another possible explanation is that our own government has a deep state program that's so top secret and underground that even the Pentagon doesn't know about it, which is also pretty freaky.

But, still, ignoring the truth doesn't make it go away, and it's bizarre that so many prominent individuals, organizations, media groups and other prominent folks and groups seem to be ignoring this.

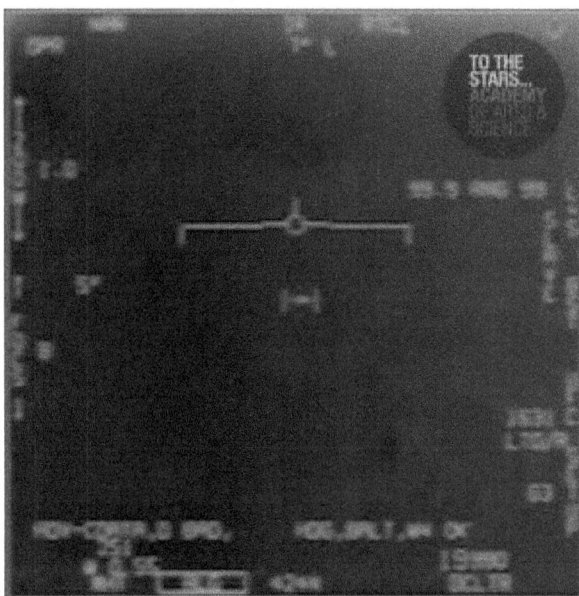

The History Channel released this video from the Pentagon showing a military jet converging on a UFO.

However, regardless of people's, and the media's, continuing to whistle in the dark, this story isn't going away.

Lawmakers have asked that the Pentagon reveal its knowledge about UFOs within six months.

The disclosure will happen, since it was included in an appropriations bill, and as we all know, money talks.

And, according to this Washington Post report, government officials in the know are saying that the information revealed will be "big."

If the revelations are as incendiary as some in the know are saying, wouldn't it be a better path for the government, and the media, to prepare the public for this, by offering a number of stories and discussions about it along the way?

Again, this is the U.S. government.

It's the Pentagon.

It's the actual military putting these stories out there to places like the New York Times and the Washington Post.

I highly doubt Ashton Kutcher is behind this.

Are we just going to ignore this?

I mean, there are some things you just can't ignore.

Ok, I lied about leaving with a punch line. Couldn't resist. Whistling in the dark and all…

You Won't BELIEVE Who Jake Paul Is fighting Next!!!

April 23rd, 2021

Jake Paul can't stop courting controversy, or people wanting to punch him in the face.

Paul has long elicited the enmity of countless people, going back to when he was on the Disney Channel series *Bizaardvark*, and pushing a rap career that saw his single, "It's Everyday Bro", become the third most disliked video in YouTube history. The hate/love relationship with Paul has continued with his boxing career, which has seen people lining up to pay in the hope of seeing him get his ass kicked.

Thus far, Paul has led a pretty charmed life in the ring, disappointing his haters.

His first bout wasn't much of a surprise result, as Paul knocked out a fellow YouTuber, AnEsonGib (known as Gib), in the first round.

Big deal. Meh.

Second bout, little bigger deal, but still, kinda meh. Paul got a second-round KO against former NBA player Nate

Robinson. Now, you look at that and think, "Hmmm… he had to fight a professional athlete." But then you look at the details, and you see that Robinson is only 5'9" tall and was probably 20 pounds lighter and with a shorter reach than Paul, and that Robinson wasn't a professional fighter, just a former pro baller who's also much older than Paul.

Paul's third fight, on the other hand, looked a lot more interesting.

He was fighting former Bellator MMA and ONE Welterweight Champion Ben Askren.

Jake Paul and Ben Askren talk about getting some wings after the fight while Mariah Carey's ex-husband looks on.

According to Askren's Wikipedia, the 36-year-old was the 2008 US Olympic Team Member and National champion and the 2005 Pan American champion in freestyle wrestling, a two–time NCAA Division I national champion (four–time finalist), and two–time Big 12 Conference champion (four–time finalist) for the Missouri Tigers, and was the second wrestler to secure multiple Dan Hodge Trophies (the wrestling equivalent of the Heisman Trophy) in folkstyle wrestling. He was also a world champion in submission wrestling.

During his time fighting MMA, he routinely got smashed in the face with fists, feet, knees and elbows by fighters far tougher and better trained than Paul.

So, of course, he "lost"* to Paul by TKO in the first round.

I put those parenthesis and asterisk there because, quite frankly, I think the fight was staged. I don't think there's any way a healthy and motivated Askren, with all his experience, would've gotten knocked out by what seemed to be a glancing blow from Paul.

I'm not alone. Many, many MMA fighters, commentators and fight fans called BS on the result of the fight, with one of the best commentary pieces being this one from sportsbible that points out Askren's inexplicably sunny demeanor after being knocked out by a YouTube star.

But, that's water, and a hefty paycheck, under the bridge.

The question now has been, who is Paul going to fight next?

He's obviously got a good thing going, and he's marketing himself in a smart way. Everyone hates/loves watching the heel in professional fighting, whether it's wrestling or MMA. They like seeing the heel, because they tune in to see the heel lose. Paul has set himself up as the heel — loud-mouthed, brash, arrogant — and it's been incredibly smart and lucrative for him. I give him credit for that. Just like I give him credit for obviously working hard to get into boxing shape. I've done that before, it's not easy; in fact, it's pretty hard work.

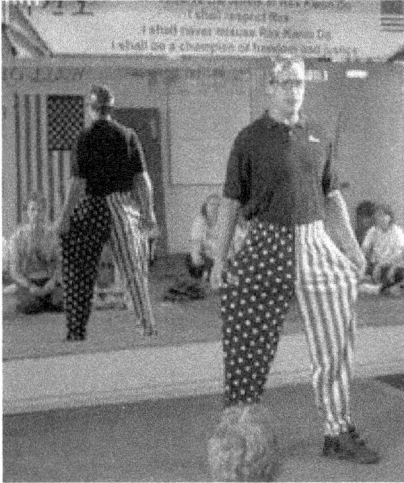

Does Jake Paul really want to get a roundhouse kick to the face from a guy wearing these bad boys?

There's been some speculation of Paul getting in the ring with someone like Floyd Mayweather or Conor McGregor, but I can't imagine that.

Both of those guys are legit champions who are closer to their peaks now than Askren was, and I can't see either, with their massive egos, signing on for an early knockout to a guy who made his bones pulling stunts on Disney channel.

No, I think Paul's next opponent needs to be someone special, someone distinct, someone who mixes sports and entertainment, who blends braggadocio and swagger just as loudly, who could step into the ring with Paul, and slap him away with little effort, all while barely getting his zubaz pants dirty.

That's right.

There's really only ONE person who should fight Jake Paul next.

And that person, of course, is Rex Kwon Do.

Rex Kwon Do kicks ass.

"Go sit over there next to Jake Paul!"

Rex Kwon Do wears a badass headband and American flag zubaz pants.

Rex Kwon Do taught Kip how to get babes.

And most of all, let us not forget that Rex Kwon Do got Starla.

Maybe Rex Kwon Do has too much experience for Paul.

After all, Rex Kwon Do spent two seasons fighting in the Octagon, and developed one of the most awesome and unbeatable systems of fighting to ever exist and be taught to pupils within an

"Sorry, Charli D'Amelio, my heart belongs to Starla!"

eight-week program.

Rex Kwon Do also has his own Wall of Honor, and his own credo:

I will respect Rex

I will not misuse Rex Kwon Do

I will be a champion of freedom and justice.

Do YOU have your own credo, Jake Paul?

I think not.

As of now, there hasn't been any serious talk about Paul facing off against Rex. Probably because he's too intimidated to consider it. But once this column gets out to my ones of readers and goes viral, once the national sports media gets ahold of this story, it's going to be to too hot to handle. The momentum will be too much to ignore, a tidal wave of fever and furor to get Paul in the ring against a REAL American hero — Rex Kwon Do!

You know you want to see it!

And so does <u>Starla</u>!

Megyn Kelly Is Like A Drunk At A Dartboard When It Comes To Her Oscars Griping

April 24th, 2021

I can't say I usually agree with former Fox News outrage mannequin Megyn Kelly, but like a drunk at a dartboard, sometimes even though her aim is off, she hits the target.

This can be seen in her latest tirade throwing red meat to the zombies looking for something to be angry about, in which she ripped on Sunday night's Oscars ceremony and its skunky ratings, saying that the Academy Awards' poor viewership numbers were because they were overly "woke."

"How's all that incessant, insufferable woke, depressing lecturing via film, interviews, social media & at the actual, awful awards show going, Hollywood?" Kelly tweeted Monday morning, in a word pizza.

And, like a pizza with too many ingredients, some of her points were good, and others were best picked off and discarded.

Now, as regular readers know, I am certainly no fan of political correctness, as it's called on the left, and "traditional values" posturing, as it's called on the right.

It's the same pandering, pearl-clutching repression under a different color umbrella to whip up support among the extremes of both sides. I find most of it ridiculous and tiresome at the very least, and at most dangerously close to subverting the intent of the first amendment. I am a fan of common sense, and logic, both of which can be utilized in most circumstances to neutralize PC/TV outrage by both the right and the left. I've written about Dr. Seuss, and Lil Nas X, and other "earth-shattering controversies" which could easily be put into perspective if people on the extremes of the right and left would just take a few deep breaths and think about things before flying into a tizzy.

The Oscar ceremony saw a precipitous dip in ratings this year. Probably because Adam Sandler and his crew didn't get any nominations for "The Wrong Missy."

A lot of people are just looking for things to be ticked off about, in large part because that outrage gets them attention and interaction, and in a world — particularly an online world — where we're becoming increasingly isolated, dehumanized, and drained of genuine connection and emotion, even rousing anger can seem preferable to the void of complete disinterest and disconnection.

That subconscious drive to connect even through clashing can be, and is, exploited for financial gain. Both Fox and MSNBC fall into predictable patterns of stoking outrage to increase their dwindling fan bases, in order to gain viewership, ratings, and advertising dollars. Without a Trump tweet or a Biden speaking gaffe of the day, they've got to stretch to make that happen. Hence, The War on Christmas, and The Battle For The Soul of Potato Head.

But what all these rushes to outrage commonly lack is perspective.

Perspective on the bigger picture, and context, of the subject they're tackling.

And that's precisely what Kelly's attack on the Oscars is lacking in the big picture. She kinda sorta hits around the target, but her desire to exploit the current outrage machine to get her attention dilutes the germane aspects of her statement.

For Kelly to accuse the Oscars' current lack of viewers on being suddenly overly woke is to ignore decades of the Academy Awards being likewise "woke" before the terminology was even a thing. It's become a cliche to talk about celebrities going onstage brandishing pet causes, going back to the 1960s and early '70s when we saw things like Marlon Brando sending Sacheen Littlefeather onstage to refuse his Oscar for "The Godfather" over the mistreatment of Native Americans and their lack of representation in Hollywood.

Be honest: How many of these movies have you actually seen? Now, also be honest: How many times have you binge watched serial killer documentaries this past year?

Hollywood's commitment to causes is nothing new at all, and has been a common theme throughout pretty much every Oscars ceremony, most of which have been highly rated.

But some of which haven't.

And the reason why this year's Academy Awards got crappy ratings can be found, in part, in the same reasons previous shows had ratings dips — BECAUSE HARDLY ANYONE SAW THE MOVIES THAT WERE NOMINATED.

There is one common thread throughout the history of Academy Awards TV ratings — if there are big, blockbuster movies nominated, the ceremony gets much bigger ratings because people are familiar with the nominees and they cheer for the films they've actually seen and liked. If the movies aren't big hits, if they're indie flicks that hardly anyone across the vast majority of the public has seen, then people don't care because they don't really feel invested in the competition. It's like me discussing who's going to win the Champions League with most Americans. "Nomadland" might as well be Manchester City.

But don't just trust me on this, let's look at actual facts and numbers. You know, those things people like to ignore when they're riling people up with ridiculous bullshit? Here's a couple paragraphs with various citations from the Wikipedia page for Academy Awards show ratings:

"Historically, the telecast's viewership is higher when box-office hits are favored to win the Best Picture award. More than 57.25 million viewers tuned to the telecast for the 70th Academy Awards in 1998, the year of *Titanic*, which generated a box office haul during its initial 1997–98 run of US$600.8 million in the US, a box office record that would remain unsurpassed for years. The 76th Academy Awards ceremony, in which *The Lord of the Rings: The Return of the King* (pre-telecast box office earnings of US$368 million) received 11 Awards

Cinemark movie theaters across the country were closed down for most of 2020, making it much more difficult for people to see and become invested in films.

including Best Picture, drew 43.56 million viewers. The most watched ceremony based on Nielsen ratings to date, however, was the 42nd Academy Awards (Best Picture *Midnight Cowboy*) which drew a 43.4% household rating on April 7, 1970.

"By contrast, ceremonies honoring films that have not performed well at the box office tend to show weaker ratings, despite how much critically acclaimed those films have been. The 78th Academy Awards which awarded low-budget independent film *Crash* (with a pre-Oscar gross of US$53.4 million) generated an audience of 38.64 million with a household rating of 22.91%. In 2008, the 80th Academy Awards telecast was watched by 31.76 million viewers on average with an 18.66% household rating, the lowest-rated and least-watched ceremony at the time, in spite of celebrating 80 years of the Academy Awards. The Best Picture winner of that particular ceremony was another independent film (*No Country for Old Men*)."

Hmmm.

So, let's try this again. Why were this year's awards so poorly rated?

Because hardly anyone saw the movies nominated for the major awards, and that's in part because ALL OF THE MOVIE THEATERS ACROSS THE COUNTRY WERE CLOSED DOWN DUE TO COVID.

Sure, people could watch films from their own homes, but it's an entirely different experience when you're renting those films through Amazon Prime, and they're not getting anywhere near as much publicity or advertising promoting them, there's not as much word-of-mouth, and they're competing against other films and entertainment which are far more flashy and attention-grabbing.

Show of hands, how many of you just flipped by "Nomadland" on the Hulu list because you didn't even know it was a movie?

You didn't even know what it was?

Well, my hand is up, at least.

The first few times I scrolled by it, I had no idea it was a major motion picture that came out this year.

I just thought it was yet another show or something that Hulu was pushing and it didn't make an immediate impression with me.

It wasn't until later, when I read our film critic Tim Brennan's review that I even knew it was a current film.

Trust me, if there had been a Tiger King movie nominated for an Oscar, people would've been intrigued. Especially if it was competing against a movie made by that bitch Carole Baskin!

In addition, over the past year of the pandemic, people have trended towards escapist fare that could take their minds off the crappy residue of life under covid. They didn't avoid these films because they were woke, they avoided them because they were serious dramas (read: depressing), which is where Kelly was kinda right in her word pizza. When I first saw the "Nomadland" promo, I thought, "Well, that looks serious and depressing… and I've already had a long, draining day… let's watch 'Seinfeld' reruns!"

I'm definitely not alone. "Tiger King," "The Last Dance," "Cobra Kai," and other pop candy has been at the top of the charts over the past year. Many pop cultural commentators, myself included, have pointed out that the absurdity and hilarity of "Tiger King" was in part tremendously resonant with people because we were at the beginning of a frightening and strange time entering a global pandemic.

Serious-minded stuff like "Nomadland" has seemed like eating steamed broccoli when you just want to get some tacos. It's not because it's woke, it's because it just seems like too much mental work to digest and maybe hits too close to home in a time when it's already depressing enough living through a pandemic.

"Nomadland" won the Oscar for Best Picture this year. How many people actually saw it?

This year's Oscar nominees were a decidedly somber bunch. There was no "Titanic," or "Lord of the Rings," or even a big hit rivalry like "Pulp Fiction" vs. "Forrest Gump."

There were just a lot of well-made, highly-crafted, quality films on serious topics.

Kind of like other "serious" films that saw a "crash" in Academy Awards ratings. (See what I did there? Thank you, thank you. Please tip your waitstaff.)

So for Megyn Kelly and others to blame the ratings plummet on "woke culture" is largely inaccurate. Yes, there's a small kernel of truth in that the seriousness of "woke culture" follows the same path as other serious topics in films which dampen viewership. But it's nothing new, it's nothing as simple as that, and it's part of a much bigger overarching trend. One which could be easily reversed next year if the theaters open up and 2021 sees a bigger array of huge box office hits that end up getting nominated.

If Kelly really wanted to say something more incisive and insightful, she would've taken aim at why the Oscars doesn't respect and laud the talents and achievements inherent in genre films (action, comedy, etc.), leaving creators to constantly turn to depressing and somber films in order to gain any critical and awards recognition.

But then again, much like the filmmakers pushing dramas to woo Academy voters, she's got to create content to appeal to her audience as well.

Other Books By Sean Leary

The Arimathean (novel)

The Blood of Destiny (novel)

Black Knight Apocalypse (novel)

Luna Death Trigger (novel)

DisIntegration (novel)

Does The Shed Skin Know It Was Once A Snake? (short stories)

Every Number Is Lucky To Someone

(short stories)

My Life As A Freak Magnet

(short stories)

Exorcising Ghosts

(graphic novel)

Here Comes The Goot!

(children's/beginning readers)

Go, Racecars, Go!

(children's/beginning readers)

Nine Little Penguin Ninjas

(children's/beginning readers)

Baby Bird

(children's/beginning readers)

We Are All Characters

(children's/beginning readers)

All My Best Adventures Are With You

(children's/beginning readers)

Beautiful Remnants of Chaotic Failures

(poetry)

Danger Maps

(poetry)

Every Broken Heart Creates The Pieces That Will Pave The Way To The Place Your Heart Will Call Home

(poetry)

Tricks of the Light

(poetry)

The Soft Venom of Promise

(poetry)

The Night Universal

(poetry)

There Is Truth In The Untamed Beat of a Heart

(poetry)

We Are Shadows In The Absence of Light

(poetry)

Magnets & Mysteries, Soft Curves & Comets

(poetry)

Infinite Sky

(poetry)

Physics & Beauty

(poetry)

Dark Equinox

(graphic novel)

The Ink In The Well

(graphic novel)

Dream States

(graphic novel)

Valentine Cords

(graphic novel)

Spyder

(graphic novel)

Sean Leary's Greatest Hits, volume one

(humor)

Sean Leary's Greatest Hits, volume two

(humor)

Sean Leary's Greatest Hits, volume three

(humor)

Sean Leary's Greatest Hits, volume four

(humor)

Sean Leary's Greatest Hits, volume five

(humor)

Sean Leary's Greatest Hits, volume six

(humor)

Sean Leary's Greatest Hits, volume seven

(humor)

Sean Leary's Greatest Hits, volume eight

(humor)

Sean Leary's Greatest Hits, volume nine

(humor)

Sean Leary's Greatest Hits, volume ten

(humor)

Sean Leary's Greatest Hits, volume eleven

(humor)

Sean Leary's Greatest Hits, volume twelve

(humor)

Your Favorite Band

(stageplay / screenplay)

Dingo Boogaloo

(stageplay / screenplay)

Rock City Live!

(stageplay / screenplay)

My Life As A Freak Magnet: The Scripts

(stageplay / screenplay)

Shots To The Heart

(stageplay)

Advice to My Son

(life stories and positive parenting)

Subliminal Cartography

(novel)

I Don't Have The Map

(poetry)

For more writing and more information, see
www.seanleary.com.

Hey, stop reading.

Go find another book, like one of those many fine Sean Leary books listed on those pages just before this one...

Enjoy the trip...

www.ingramcontent.com/pod-product-compliance
Lightning Source LLC
Chambersburg PA
CBHW020851090426
42736CB00008B/335